Flotsam

Flotsam

John Stewart

PAUL DRY BOOKS

Philadelphia   2010

First Paul Dry Books Edition, 2010

Paul Dry Books, Inc.
Philadelphia, Pennsylvania
www.pauldrybooks.com

Text type: Fairfield Light
Display type: Bodoni and Avenir
Designed and composed by P. M. Gordon Associates

1 3 5 7 9 8 6 4 2
Printed in the United States of America

Library of Congress Cataloging-in-Publication Data
Stewart, John, 1919–
  Flotsam / John Stewart. — 1st Paul Dry Books ed.
      p. cm.
  ISBN 978-1-58988-063-4 (alk. paper)
  1. Stewart, John, 1919—Aesthetics. 2. Photographers—
Great Britain—Biography. I. Title.
  TR140.S688A3 2010
  770.92—dc22
  [B]
                                            2010024157

For my son, Nicolas

CONTENTS

How wondrous, how mysterious!
I carry fuel, I draw water.

Layman P'ang Chu-Shih

PREFACE

Few of us live our lives with an avowed purpose. I envy those blessed with it. I envy the clarity of their goals as much as their resolve. Whether the avowed purpose arises in youth or in middle years, their lives are worthy of record. For the rest of us drifters, there's one question we can each ask: Is it possible to detect a thread running through our existence, a thread that does not necessarily lead anywhere, but at least serves, even occasionally, as a beacon, an indication, a reminder? I am referring to the constant inner voice, to the presence of a faithful compass needle. That perception, when it exists, also warrants a record.

"May you live in interesting times," says the Chinese curse. Times of war and upheaval prevent the sage from living as he should. I lived through a good part of the twentieth century, and I've had an interesting life, or so I'm often told. That may be, but try as I may, I'm unable to trace its thread, and even less an avowed purpose. I perceive a succession of events, experiences, and states of being. Yes, occasionally I've touched something here or there. Such a moment occurred during the Second World War, when, as a very young soldier, I was a prisoner of the Japanese. I had been sentenced to death. As

I knelt in front of the officer who, sword drawn, was making a first pass over my head, I experienced what I understood much later to be a moment of "being awake." Within the few seconds between the certainty that I was about to be beheaded and the knowledge that I wouldn't, I realized that I was "a machine." The words in quotation marks are not mine, but Gurdjieff's (about whom more later). However brief the experience, it resulted eventually in what is known as a sea-change, although it was not immediately perceptible that the vector of my existence had been set at a slightly different angle. Still, most of the time, as I've said, I have been out of touch. But who is this "I"? Or rather, which of the "I"s are we talking about, the variegated, contradictory beings who play different roles on different stages?

History necessarily must lead to a conclusion, more precisely to an explicative theory (why the empire expanded, why it declined), or else you're left with analects. That's what I have attempted to put down in this book—analects, a variety of anecdotes. As there's no thread, they are presented in no order, save at the beginning when they follow a simple chronology to help the reader make his or her way into this miscellany.

Paris, 2010

Flotsam (flŏt səm) n. 1. Such part of the wreckage of a ship or its cargo as is found floating on the surface of the sea. 2. Discarded odds and ends; bits and pieces.

Working Days

Proletarian

Three months after my birth in London, I was transported to Paris where my father headed the French branch of the family business, at the time the world's foremost company of office copying machines. Convinced that one day I was destined to take over from him, he saw to it that I received a French education. His father-in-law, my grandfather and founder of the company—London, 1881—disagreed: "John will never be in the family business: He's the artist among us." I was then four years old. I once mentioned that remarkable foresight to a friend who raised hounds. "Nothing surprising," he remarked. "When I look at my pups, I know exactly how they'll turn up."

My oracular grandfather wasn't listened to, and the time came when "a decision" had to be made. I had no vocation, nor did I want to pursue my studies. Business, any business, would do, it was decided on my behalf. The French phase was over, real life was in England, and that's where I was to be shipped off. It was summer's end, and we were in our house on the Normandy coast. My mother addressed me sternly: "You're leaving us in a couple of days. I don't think

I've really done what I should have to get you ready for life. So tomorrow morning, Dominique, who's in charge of linens, will show you how to iron a pair of trousers. In the afternoon Cook will teach you to make a decent omelet."

The year was 1938. Britain and Germany were preparing to get at each other's throat, but this was no reason to impede business transactions, and an uncle of mine was at the time involved in a very odd one. The British armed forces were lacking a specialized lubricating oil. The Germans had both the technique and the plants. German Jews had the money. A deal was struck: the Germans would ship over the refinery and erect it in Britain, while the German Jews would foot the bill—to be refunded in Sterling if they ever managed to emigrate to Britain. In effect, the bottom line was that German know-how would allow British tanks and aircraft to be properly lubricated for the inevitable conflict, while Britain might never have to pay for the refinery. The ethical niceties of the situation are worth pondering.

The uncle found me a job at the refinery, in Manchester, a grim manufacturing town in the north of England. By the time I presented myself for work, construction was well under way. The shiny, bulbous cracking towers were looming above the Manchester Ship Canal, a desolate industrial landscape under a permanent drizzle. The English manager introduced me to the boss of the German team, a slim, ultra-blond and hard-faced young woman engineer. She was dressed in black and wore knee-high black boots. Over her left breast, she had pinned a discreet swastika. All that was needed to complete the outfit was a riding crop. In a pernicious way, I found her irresistible. Or was it the impossible challenge— the celebrated *goût de l'étranger*? Of course I got nowhere and tried to console myself with the local girls whose Mancunian accent I found a perfect libido killer.

One of my family's precepts is that "You start at the bottom." After my French lycée and the final exam and a B.A. in philosophy, I found myself suddenly relegated to the lowest rung of the British proletariat. I joined a team of seven workers—two welders, two fitters, and three navvies, the unskilled men whose brawn was needed to handle steel pipes. I was to start as an apprentice navvy. We dug ditches in the soggy soil and laid down large steel ducts, which the skilled members of the team then welded together.

My connection with management was surely no secret, yet no one ever alluded to it. I never heard a snide remark, not even a reference to the class struggle. Could it have been dormant in Lancashire? The reason for the team's acceptance, I believe, was the test I successfully faced on my first day at work—I drank the revolting brew of sweet tea I was offered. I should elaborate: Each man owned a billycan, and as he left home his wife handed him half-a-dozen "screws." These were square pieces of newspaper in which the wife had deposited a gooey mixture of sweet condensed milk, sugar, and tea leaves, with the paper twisted in the shape of a screw. The team laid down tools every hour, each man filled his billycan with water, got the welders to bring it to a boil, and with a grimy finger scraped the content of the screw into it. I have yet to decide whether that tea ordeal was worse than others I've had to face in the course of years. I think the accolade must go to Tibetan tea and its rancid yak butter laced with salt and soda. It's no rarity to discover a few yak hairs floating in your Tibetan bowl, just as fragments of the local newspaper were not unusual in the Lancashire billycan.

I lasted three months, although two weeks after joining my team I was judged to be no longer an apprentice navvy, but a fully-fledged one. Manchester was dismal, the work brutal, my life unutterably dull. I threatened desertion. I called my parents in Paris. I called the uncle responsible for my plight. I was told to hold on. Presently, a job was found with the Roth-schild bank in London.

Gentleman

Merchant-banker in the City of London was an attractive prospect in spite of my repeated failure as a schoolboy to keep accounts of my pocket money and my father's resultant ire and indictment.

My new employers, deeming it necessary that I acquire some knowledge in the workings of stocks and bonds, handed me over to a firm of friendly stockbrokers, Messrs. Hirsch, Stokes & Wilson. First, I had to be vetted: admission to the floor of the London Stock Exchange was as selective as to a good club. Mr. Stokes was my sponsor as I presented myself before the committee, somber looking men seated around a large horseshoe desk. Portraits in oil, presumably of the stock exchange's ancestors, hung on the paneled walls. I stood in the U of the horseshoe desk, Mr. Stokes sat by my side in an armchair. The atmosphere was hushed.

The interrogation got under way. Father's occupation, schooling, and sports—mainly sports. Did I ride to hounds, did I shoot, sail, play golf . . . Finally I was requested to leave the room and wait outside. After no more than five minutes, Mr. Stokes came out and nodded to me to return and face the committee. "Don't make a fool of yourself," said the chairman. Nothing more. He meant, I suppose, "Don't let us catch you with your hand in the till." I was admitted.

Mr. Stokes led me to one of the underground bars around the House, as the stock exchange is referred to, where we celebrated the event over a glass of champagne. I also got my basic training. A stiff collar was compulsory as well as a flower in my button hole (not a rose, worn mostly by the older members, and really acceptable only if you grew it yourself).

I was never to use the few wooden benches built around the pillars of the House; they were reserved for ancient members who, although retired, needed to get away from their wives. I was light years away from my mates at the Manchester Oil Refinery, yet I would find myself once more on the lowest rung of those allowed on the floor of the House: I was a Blue Button, for such was the insignia I wore on the lapel of my jacket. A Blue Button wasn't allowed to trade, even on behalf of his employers. Basically, he could make enquiries about the price of shares but not much else. With my knowledge of French, however, I was to be trained in arbitrage with Brussels. More about that later.

Before we parted, Mr. Stokes presented me to the doormen who, in their top hats and blue uniforms, mounted guard over the several doors giving access to the House. They were known as Waiters, for trading in shares had first taken place in coffee houses. These Waiters memorized the faces of people entitled to enter the House. Once or twice a year someone managed to get past them. When discovered, the call went up, "Stranger in the House!" All trading stopped, and the culprit was expelled.

I'd rented a small studio in a contemporary apartment building of striking design. It had a swimming pool, as well as tennis and squash courts. I had to present myself at the House by 10 A.M., when continental bourses opened, and I was back home by 5 P.M. I stood around the House, reading the paper or chatting until the number 27 lit up on a given panel hanging high up on one of the walls. It signaled a telephone call from Brussels. The price of a share traded both in London and Brussels had suddenly moved up or down, perhaps enough to warrant buying in one market and selling simultaneously in the other. Such is the nature of arbitrage. I sat in my phone booth, cradling a bulky, finger-driven calculator, or else a slide rule, and worked currency exchanges and costs of transfer, finally instructing one of my firm's people to buy or sell a number of shares.

An old friend of my family was the honorary colonel of a company in the Territorial Army, a peacetime military body of volunteers. The unit in question was an officer-producing unit, meaning that in time we'd all receive the King's commission, that is, become officers. The company manned searchlights. It numbered three hundred men, of whom around a third came from the stock exchange, another third from the law courts, the rest being a mixture of punters, racing men, and the like. We were all privates, or rather sappers, as the unit was part of the Royal Engineers. (Evelyn Waugh in *Men at Arms* refers to it as "a territorial search-light battery manned entirely by fashionable aesthetes who were called 'the monstrous regiment of gentlemen.'" That appellation, however, was pure Waugh invention.) I had no choice, of course, than to join 332 Company. One evening a week, we took our searchlights to Regent's Park and tried to catch in our beam a slow de Havilland Gipsy Moth plane sent up by the RAF. To help us, we used a device called a sound locator, which could detect the aircraft's position in the night sky by focusing on the sound of the engine. We found the device far more effective when we directed it toward the park's bushes and heard, vastly amplified, the happy sounds of people engaged in fornication.

In early spring 1939, the company was sent to Suffolk for a month of more ambitious training. I fell in love with rural England, its villages and country pubs. Then, back in London one morning in late July, seeing the number 27 light up, I went to the phone booth and heard "Camden Arms," which was the password for mobilization. Other young men had received an identical message. All transactions stopped. A very ancient member, with a face like an apple that had

been left too long in a drawer, and on his head a top hat green with age, shook my hand: "I saw them go off like this in 1914. Look at my eyes. You'll come back alive, my boy. God bless." I went home, packed a suitcase, put on my uniform, called a cab, and reported to barracks.

2

War Stories

The "fashionable aesthetes" of my section (we were nine all told) manned a searchlight close to the village of Finchingfield in Essex. We were housed in a hideous Quonset hut, but our austere army rations were supplemented by regular shipments of rarefied foods from Fortnum & Mason in London, and our uniforms were "bespoke," mine cut by my tailor on Dover Street. Each month I received my cigarettes from Fribourg & Treyer—of Virginia and Turkish tobacco and made to order. One by one, members of the section were advised that they had become officers and left us—for a fashionable regiment, it was hoped. Such was the snobbish and sybaritic life we led until *la drôle de guerre* came to an end.

I was not one of those who received an immediate commission but was eventually ordered to present myself at the War Office in London. I've told* how I was transferred from searchlights to the Intelligence Corps, and why in October 1941 I was on my way to the Middle East, along with the

---

* *To the River Kwai—Two Journeys, 1943, 1979*, Bloomsbury, London, 1988.

twelve other men of the 15th Field Security Section, trained in counter-espionage and, as the name implies, military security. We all spoke a smattering of Arabic and had been briefed about the countries we'd been assigned to, Egypt and Iran. Captain L., our commanding officer, had seen service in the Cairo Police. He was now returning to his old haunts, and this had prompted him to pack a dinner jacket in his trunk. Our journey took three months (and troopships, remember, are a noisome means of travel) because German U-boats blocked access to the Mediterranean. We crossed the North Atlantic, then the South, and steamed round the tip of Africa. Finally we sailed north toward Port Said, stopping on the way to refuel at Mombasa, on Africa's east coast. There, orders were received from London to divert the ship to Singapore as the Imperial Japanese Army was fast making its way down the Malay Peninsula. Our Middle East training would be of little use in that theater of war, and Captain L. approached the Major-General in charge of the 18th Division, who was on board the *Mount Vernon*. Would he grant the Field Security Section permission to disembark and make its way overland to Egypt? No problem, said the general. What about my dinner jacket? asked the Captain, for his trunk was in the ship's hold. No question of emptying the hold for that, replied the general. In that case, concluded the captain, we'll go to Singapore, extract it, and make our way to Egypt. Now you know why two-thirds of his section perished in Japanese POW camps.

Dreams

Dreaming is often an escape from waking days that are hard to bear. Such was our experience when, after the fall of Singapore in February 1942, we found ourselves prisoners of the Japanese. For the Allies, it was also the war's direst moment:

The Germans occupied most of Europe and were rolling up the Soviet armies; Rommel and the Afrikakorps were close to Cairo; the American fleet had been badly mauled at Pearl Harbor; and the Philippines, along with all of Southeast Asia, were in Japanese hands. As for Singapore, the "impregnable fortress" had collapsed in one week. Yet rumors of a very different kind were being heard in Changi, where British and Australian prisoners had been assembled. (Changi, once the site of British Army barracks, was a vast area in the eastern tip of Singapore Island.) Rumors told of an Allied landing in France, Russian armies pushing their way toward Germany, North Africa secure in British hands. Strangely, no one seemed to notice that the Japanese were suffering no defeats. The reason, of course, was simple. They were the originators of these rumors. Maybe they believed that happy prisoners—"Home by Christmas" was our mantra of hope—would be less likely to try to escape; or maybe when we learned the truth, despondency would make us docile.

A few radios had been successfully smuggled into Changi, but only key personnel were in the know. Possession of a radio was punishable by death, and had war news been bandied about, the Japanese would soon have traced its origin. I was privileged, and knew what was happening. Hence didn't share the euphoria of most prisoners. Clearly, it would take a very long time for the Allies to get the upper hand, if ever they could.

Getting back to dreams. We dreamed of all things we were deprived of—food, sex, family—reminders of the good life we'd left behind and of the good days that, we hoped, would return. My own dreams fitted the usual pattern, save for one, which both in form and substance was singular. It dealt neither with the present nor with the past. It didn't project a better future, but was flat, uneventful, and unequivocal. It was disembodied: no figure appeared, no one spoke, no visual background became manifest. Yet the information it conveyed was overwhelmingly clear: YOU WILL BE A PRISONER FOR THREE AND A HALF YEARS.

I never told anyone about the dream. To share it would have whittled its secret power. I could not dismiss it. At its prime level, it was a promise of survival. But I must have been vouchsafed momentarily a special wisdom, for I didn't see it as a guarantee. I'd rolled the dice, I'd shuffled the cards, they'd come up with the big prize—life. But there would be no sitting back and waiting. I had to justify the dream, *I had to play the game*, and play it to the end.*

Staying alive meant acquiring a rare skill that would make me, if not indispensable, at least not readily expendable. Among the 120,000 Allied prisoners, there were only seven who could speak Japanese, most of them sons of missionaries brought up in Japan. I resolved to learn *Nippon-go*, the language of our captors, and I made arrangements for daily lessons with two of those Japanese-speakers. I have little doubt that my work as interpreter was the main reason for my survival.

---

* Once, but only once, I left the gaming table. It happened during the forced marches to the Burma border. Wracked by malaria and dysentery, oozing blood, desperately weak, legs giving up, I left the column of prisoners and laid myself down on a thicket of fern, and waited for death. But the gods dispatched their messenger. Out of nowhere appeared a barefoot Thai balancing on his head a bunch of tiny bananas. He looked at me. Our eyes met. Not a word was uttered but he placed the bananas at my side. I gave him old shorts I carried in my backpack, and he left. I devoured the whole bunch. I tried standing up and let out a tremendous fart that reverberated in the bamboo forest. Evil had been let out. Strength renewed, I made my way to the next staging area. There I found the column of 300 men, collapsed, fast asleep, sprawled helter-skelter in the mud, as if victims of sudden and instant death.

A Book, a Film, a Myth

Had it not been for the movie *The Bridge on the River Kwai*, the "Death Railway," a mere blip in the history of the Second World War, would by now be utterly forgotten. The film is based on a French author's hearsay about Japanese POW camps; by a director with a personal and doubtful message he wished to convey; about a river that was never called "Kwai." These are the ingredients of the myth offered at Kanchanaburi, a town west of Bangkok and the site of a steel bridge that substitutes for the wooden bridge of both book and movie (the latter, incidentally, shot in Sri Lanka). The river's name is the Nam Kwae Noi, but for tourist reasons it has been officially renamed Kwai. The two military cemeteries are a pious sham. The dead were cremated in situ, and all that remained of them were anonymous ashes and bones moved to the cemeteries long after the war. In brief, Kanchanaburi has become a major tourist attraction with its obligatory *son et lumière*, a museum, souvenir shops, and river rides. Happily, a project submitted a few years ago to recreate a POW camp with re-enactors impersonating sadistic Japanese guards and hungry prisoners was quashed.

 Pierre Boulle, author of the book that inspired the movie, had a message: War is madness. David Lean, the film's director, had another interpretation: a professional soldier, he believed, is an incipient criminal. Moreover, the premise of both book and film is the Japanese Army Engineers' inability to build a wooden bridge across a river three hundred feet wide without Western expertise. That was of course nonsense. Our captors needed prisoners for slave labor. And a senior British officer who collaborated with the Japanese, as Nicholson does in the movie, would have been quickly removed by his fellow officers.

Such then is the way reality becomes myth. A myth is a story that everyone knows; its connection with the original source matters little. Just as a relic, be it a saint's bone, a hair from Muhammad's head, or a tooth from the Buddha's mouth, is a fiction housed in an extravagant temple, the bridge at Kanchanaburi has become "The Bridge on the River Kwai" relic. If Pierre Boulle had a specific bridge in mind for his novel, every indication points to the bridge at Sonkrai, my old camp 200 miles north. However, it would be well to keep in mind that in the course of the 258 miles of track on the Siam-Burma Railway there are 688 bridges.

Foujita

No more than a month after Singapore's surrender, I was in Changi, that vast area where British and Australian prisoners had been assembled, when someone came to see me with surprising news. "Foujita is in the camp!"

Foujita had been one of the most singular and boisterous figures of the Paris art scene between the two wars. In Montparnasse, he was one of Kiki's most famous lovers, pursued by women and success, above all a strikingly original painter of cats and women. Hubert, my childhood friend, had Marie Laurencin teach him painting (whereas my master was a saintly and obscure Jewish artist), and Marie Laurencin was at the time one of Foujita's lovers. Even as a small boy, I knew Foujita for his pranks, for his round eyeglasses, and for his strange haircut that dropped right above his eyebrows.

When I found him strolling in the camp, I introduced myself, mentioning my acquaintance with Marie Laurencin. Foujita was wearing a paramilitary Japanese Army uniform. He was delighted to speak French—it was the first thing he mentioned when we met. The second was, "*Mon pauvre ami, I'm not going to ask you what you're doing here . . .*"

I replied by asking him, in turn, what he was doing in that strange uniform.

"Well, I thought I was French, or at least that I was going to spend the rest of my life in Paris," said Léonard Foujita (he'd assumed that first name for the great Leonardo), "but when the Germans arrived in Paris, Tokyo sent them a signal, 'Ship Foujita back to Japan.' It took me three months by way of South America to return to my native land. When I got there, they said to me, 'You're an official war artist.' Now, what can I do for you?"

He couldn't do much, but I did ask him for drawing materials. Poor Foujita, I thought, having to sketch miserable and famished prisoners rather than delicious cats and languorous women.

But poor Foujita showed himself to be exceedingly versatile. He turned out paintings of furious battles and banzai charges, and a documentary shows him on board a Japanese aircraft carrier, sitting in front of his easel during the Battle of Midway in June 1942. True, his father had been a general, but in spite of his love of France he held extreme militaristic views during the war. When in 1949 he decided to return to Paris via the United States, the Americans refused him entry. The French saw his war episode differently. The conflict in the Pacific was geographically and emotionally so distant that it was of no import. In 1957, he was awarded the Legion of Honor. Two years later, he converted to Catholicism. He died in Switzerland in 1968.

Friends and Strange Encounters

A soldier always needs a friend—a "buddy" in the US forces, a "cobber" in the Australian, a "mate" in the British. Mine was Martin McCall, an Irishman from the local volunteer force, the Malay Regiment. He'd served in the legal service of the Federated Malay States as Assistant Deputy Prosecutor in Kuala Lumpur, and one had better never be on McCall's wrong side. His tongue lashings were instant and scathing. One evening when we were playing poker, one of us, an Australian, kept objecting that whatever was happening was not "according to Hoyle" (*Hoyle's Rules* being the poker man's bible). McCall turned on him, "None of your marsupial manners with us, please."

McCall got his comeuppance a few days later as we were strolling down a road in Changi, and from afar we saw a covey of Japanese staff officers walking in our direction. We stood to the side of the road and bowed deeply as they went by. A major left the group and strode up to Martin, sword rattling against his polished boots. "Good afternoon, Mister McCall. A pleasure meeting you here. I trust you are keeping well," said the major, who then turned on his heels and rejoined his peers.

Martin's face turned white. The major had been his barber in prewar Kuala Lumpur—in truth a Japanese secret agent, the barbershop serving as his cover. His knowledge of English at the time had seemed rudimentary, and Martin, no doubt, had communicated with him in pidgin English, treating him in the offhand manner usual at that time when dealing with "natives."

•

Changi turned out to be a holiday camp when compared to the conditions in the working camps along the River Kwai and beyond. Sonkrai, where I spent the longest period, had the worst reputation and suffered the most casualties. Cholera, dysentery, beriberi, and malaria were fast depleting the original contingent of 1,800 prisoners. By war's end, only 182 were still alive. The Japanese were merciless. Anyone who could stand up had to work. Even "the gondoliers," as we named them—who couldn't stand up but were fit enough to drag themselves through the mud with the help of bamboo poles—were sent to the bridge. In the struggle to survive, men formed small groups. One such group I'd never paid much attention to was made up of Dutch prisoners, and one day four of them came to see me. They were Jews they told me, and their rabbi wished to speak to me. The rabbi looked like any other prisoner—ribs sticking out through the remnant of an army shirt, feet in clogs hacked out of old tires. He addressed me in Yiddish, and I told him I didn't understand him.

"But you are Jewish?" asked the rabbi.

I confirmed his guess.

"What kind of a Jew are you?" said the rabbi switching to English. "You speak Japanese and you don't understand Yiddish?"

Yom Kippur was taking place the following week and the Dutchmen wanted me to approach Lieutenant Abe, the Japanese Engineers' ferocious commanding officer, with the request to excuse them from duty on that day. I told them I would do nothing of the kind. Every man who could stand up had to work, not only on order of the Japs, but because the sick received no rations and the workers had to share their food with them. Lieutenant Abe, I added, was likely not to give a hoot about Jews.

Yet I met one Japanese who did. He was a major on a tour of inspection. I had been told to show him the two-tier bridge we were building to accommodate both road and rail. He left his Marmon lorry by the track, and on the way through the half-mile of jungle paths that led to the bridge, he revealed that he'd become an expert on a subject that few Japanese cared about—the Jews. "I've studied them and their history, and now I can smell a Jew ten meters away."

I did nothing to disprove his claim.

We reached the bridge at noon when the prisoners were allowed half an hour's rest and a mug of hot water. One of the Japanese Engineers blew his whistle, and about a hundred men emerged stark naked from the river where they had been working on the pilings. Many, as is not unusual in Britain, were circumcised. The major couldn't get over his surprise.

"I never knew you had so many Jews in the British Army," he remarked.

I did nothing to dispel his belief.

Salt

The monsoon turned the road into a muddy rut. Trucks were stranded, bullock-carts took over, but they, too, soon foundered on the trail. No food could reach us, so the Japanese released one elephant from the work pool. That was insufficient. An adult male can carry no more than three hundred pounds on his back, including its mahout, who complained that the mud was too deep and his reward too thin. Every other day, parties of fifty men, mostly officers, were sent on foot beyond the Three Pagoda Pass, where supplies were brought down from Burma rather than coming up from Thailand. These men carried rice for the twelve hundred prisoners at Sonkrai. (Six hundred had perished in three months—lean days, when obsession with food snuffed out common humanity.) Crime became prevalent. We hunted snakes, collected grubs and insects, attempted to trap small animals such as rats and monkeys, but in vain. Feeding off the jungle is a full-time job. One of our officers had been a rubber planter before the war, and he knew the Sakais, the indigenous, pigmy-like inhabitants of the Malay forests. To ensure an evening meal, he told us, the whole family started gathering food at first light. Unlike the Sakais, however, we had nothing to deposit at the foot of trees and expect the following day to find a bag of salt brought by traders in exchange for jungle products. Salt—because Martin McCall and I suffered from an excruciating itch, waking up at night in a frenzy of scratching, and when we reported to our medical officer, we were told, "Salt deficiency, nothing to do about it."

I thought otherwise. The Japanese had an ample supply of salt, and we had none. I cut off a six-inch length of thin bamboo and punched out the inner wood membrane, ending up with a smooth tube, one end sharpened to a point. The tool snug in my pocket, I went to the Japanese cookhouse and asked the cook to help me with a problem of linguistics. He was pleased to be thought a scholar. From the start of the lesson I stood leaning against the bags of salt piled up along a wall. Hand in pocket, I jammed the sharp end of the bamboo into a bag. The salt trickled down the tube, and the lesson was made to last until my pocket filled up. Thanking the cook for his trouble, I returned triumphantly to our part of the camp.

Away from prying eyes, Martin and I savored the heavenly substance. Night fell, and with it the terrible, unabated itch. The effect isn't instantaneous, said the medical officer the next morning, yet three days later there was no improvement. I mentioned our lack of success to a sergeant major. His diagnosis differed from the doctor's. "If I may say so," he told me, "because you and your friend are gentlemen you probably haven't bothered to look for lice. But I would if I were you."

We did, and discovered that our shorts had become a suitable, if overcrowded, habitat for the vermin. We had to keep up our amour-propre, so ours were "bamboo lice," whereas everyone else had common, ordinary lice. When evening came and we were off duty, Martin and I slipped off our shorts, crouched around the fire, picked our lice between thumb and index finger, and dropped them gleefully into the embers.

Toyoyama

Of all the guards on the Siam-Burma Railway, the most feared and the most hated was a Korean auxiliary, a *gunzoku* named Toyoyama. As soon as he heard I was the interpreter, he whacked me with his golf club. He hit me on the side of the head, and I fell on the ground. Light exploded in my eyes, a shooting pain flooded my head. Instantly, I was filled with a rage that never left me.

We'd just got off a five-day train journey from Singapore, so tightly jammed in cattle cars that we had to take turns just to sit down. Over the entrance of the camp in Bampong, the southern base of the railway we were sent to build, a panel announced TRANSIT CAMP FOR CATTLE, COOLIES AND PRISONERS OF WAR. That is where Toyoyama and I first met. He ruled over that foul place with its open latrines crawling with maggots, its air filled with huge green flies, and its lice-infested huts. Lieutenant Fukuda, his lover, was nominally the camp commandant, but he was under the Korean's spell, as he would be later in the work camps south of the Three Pagoda Pass.

Whenever a new arrival of prisoners was expected, Toyoyama stood at the camp's entrance, golf club in hand, always immaculately dressed, lithe, hyperactive, and dangerous. He exuded a strong sexual aura. His skin, matte and pale, was as smooth as a woman's. His eyes were constantly in motion, darting over the prisoner he was about to hit, as if searching for the spot that would bring the greatest pain. His voice at times reached the heights of a coloratura, at others it turned into a hiss.

His portrait,* taken in a Singapore prison after the war, shows a young and beautiful human being, a male face subtly verging on the female. The mouth could be a girl's, and the two sides of his face seem to present a perfect symmetry. Toyoyama had the attributes of the fallen angel.

After Japan surrendered, I was ordered to remain in Singapore and help round up IJA personnel who had mistreated prisoners in unacceptable ways. Out of sight, a number of Australians settled their accounts with some Japanese guards who'd been particularly unpleasant, but nothing much was said about it. The Japanese garrison on Singapore Island had been disarmed, and regrouped across the causeway in the jungle areas of Johore Bahru, there to await news of its fate. That became my hunting ground. My superior was an infantry major, a fierce individual with an array of service ribbons on his chest. We moved around, the major and I in one jeep, six Ghurka riflemen in the other. We interrogated those Japanese units that had served on the railway and were surprised by the cooperation, even the docility, of the Japanese soldiery.

I had but one aim—to find Toyoyama and kill him.

At last, one morning, I learned that Toyoyama was attached to a company of engineers, and I gave orders to produce him for my return at 10:00 A.M. the following day. I told the major I wanted to be alone for this confrontation. He understood: I was going to shoot Toyoyama, and I didn't want any witnesses. He'd wait with the Ghurkas for my return.

At precisely ten o'clock, Toyoyama was brought out of a tent by two Japanese NCOs. He saw me but showed neither sign of recognition nor surprise. Instead of the statutory bow which I'd practiced for so long, and was mandatory in

* Robin Rowland, *A River Kwai Story: The Sonkrai Tribunal*, Allen and Unwin, Crows Nest, NSW, Australia, 2007.

the IJA from a lower rank to a higher, he nodded his head. As if impelled by a will of its own, my right hand moved to my revolver in its thigh holster. Simultaneously, as if I'd stood some distance away, I saw the image of these two men, standing a few paces from one another, linked in a past that had turned full circle. Drained of all feeling, I sensed a void, an absence rather than a loss, like the flame that ceases to be after you've blown out the candle. Hate, resentment, and desire for revenge were no more. I told a Japanese officer present that I would have Toyoyama picked up in the coming days.

"How did it go?" asked the Major when I returned to the jeep. "Did you shoot him?"

"No."

"I understand. Not easy, point blank with a handgun. Why don't you get one of the Ghurkas' carbines and shoot the little shit from twenty feet away?"

"No, Sir. I don't want to shoot him."

"What? After all you've told me? The Japs have done a fucking good job on your head! You're not a man anymore."

A year later, I received a letter from a brigadier-general in the legal department of the British Army. He'd visited Toyoyama in prison. At his trial, the Korean had recognized and apologized for his crimes, and that was no doubt what saved him from the gallows. He was an exemplary prisoner, the general was told, selfless, attentive to other men's troubles, and ready with solace and encouragement. (He served his sentence, was freed in 1955, and returned to Korea.)

More recently, I received an e-mail from a Canadian historian* working on the trial of the IJA personnel at Sonkrai. At his trial, Toyoyama had tried to exonerate Lieutenant Fukuda, whereas Fukuda hadn't lifted a finger to come to the

---

* *A River Kwai Story*, op. cit.

defense of his military inferior. Did I have an idea why, questioned the Canadian historian. I responded with two tentative ideas.

To escape the opprobrium of their origins, Koreans in the Japanese forces followed (or pretended to follow) the ways of Bushido, the code of the Japanese warrior. I suggested that Toyoyama might have been imbued with the rule of *nimmu*, the obligation to repay your debt to your superiors be they your parents, your teacher, or, in this case, your officer. The obligation, however only worked one way. On the other hand, Toyoyama's attitude might have been dictated by the two men's sexual and emotional involvement. We shall never know.

•

Yes, I was a prisoner for three-and-a-half years, just as the dream had predicted. But in 2006, as I was working on a French translation of the book I'd written about life and death on the River Kwai, I tried to figure out how close to the reality the dream had actually come. Multiplying 365 days by 3.5 came to 1,276 days (take or leave a few hours). I then worked out precisely how much time had elapsed from 16 February 1942, the morning after the capitulation of Singapore when I heard I was a prisoner, to 21 August 1945, the day when Colonel Banno of the Imperial Japanese Army saluted me. It came to 1,275 days, off by one day, until I remembered that 1944 was a leap year.

3

Discovering Photography

Shortly after my repatriation from the Far East, I went to New York where, after a period of seesawing between France, England, and America, I decided to settle down, for a while anyway, in Manhattan. My first job was writing articles on Asia for the *Columbia Gazetteer of the World* and its *Encyclopedia*, but unsuited for the academic life, I subsequently went to work for the American outlet of a British publisher. That job lasted a year. Two unfortunate encounters led me to look for another occupation. The first occurred on a trip back to England when I had to call on a lady who was writing a book of memoirs. She lived in Suffolk, in her Elizabethan manor. At dinner, she sat at one end of a long refectory table, I at the other. The meal over, the butler deposited a decanter of port by my side. I stood up to serve my hostess, making my way along the right side of the table when I heard her icy voice, "Young man, port travels on the LEFT!" She requested that my employers assign another editor for her memoirs.

The second encounter was with a psychoanalyst and author who lived in New Jersey. I was asked to wait in the living room when his four-year old son pushed the door open, climbed on the piano—the lid was open—and peed into it.

I was trying to put a stop to this behavior, my voice several decibels above normal, when the father appeared. He threw me out of the house, screaming, "I hope for their sakes that you never have children!" He withdrew his manuscript and moved to another publisher. It was suggested by my employers that perhaps I was not suited to deal with the vagaries of authors. Eventually, I realized that I needed to be on my own. Taking orders went against the grain. Maybe I had not entirely recovered from six years in the army.

I got married to a very young woman born in Paris of Russian parents. Natacha urged me to think seriously about our future. It was spring, and I suggested the Colombe d'Or, a small but celebrated country hotel and restaurant in the Provençal village of St. Paul de Vence—a pleasant place to think. Natacha agreed. I acquired a camera (at the time I didn't own one), a Leica. I'd long admired its design, the silky white metal and the sexy black body. Anyway, who knew, I might want to take a few pictures.

We first flew to London, where I had arranged to pick up a two-seater, black MG with big nickel-chrome headlights and a wooden steering wheel. After crossing the Channel, we slowly motored down to St. Paul, following country roads (autoroutes were to come much later), and a week after leaving London we pulled up at the door of the Colombe d'Or. We met Paul Roux, the owner. He was sitting at a table in the garden, a broad-rimmed hat from the Camargue region on his head, a blue peasant smock over his shirt. Feathery white doves fluttered down from the roof, ruffling the warm sunny air with the beating of their wings. When told we wanted to stay at his place for a month or perhaps two, Monsieur Roux asked to know why. I explained that it was to decide what to do with my life. "I suppose you don't have much money," he said, his voice lowering as if he was thinking aloud. The Colombe d'Or was anything but a modest, moderately priced country inn. Moreover, Roux was choosy about his guests. He would shelter artists in exchange for their works; or he might tell someone who rolled up in a Rolls Royce, but whose face or manners he disliked, that the inn was full. In our case, he suggested bed and board for the equivalent of five dollars a day—a giveaway—moreover allotting us one of the few rooms with a bathroom. A Matisse painting hung over the bed.

Over drinks at the bar before dinner, Roux introduced us to the intellectual and artistic fauna that congregated there daily, among them André Verdet, a poet. Within minutes, Verdet and I were addressing one another with the familiar *tu* rather than the formal *vous*. Perhaps because I was a foreigner, he divulged a *crise de conscience*, a moral dilemma. He loved abstract painting, but he also had a great deal of sympathy with the Communist movement—in the early 1950s, a universal tendency in French intellectual circles. The orthodox Communists despised abstract art; only socialist realism directed by Moscow was acceptable. If, thanks in small part to his efforts, pondered Verdet, the Communists ever came to power, what would happen to him and his collection of abstract art? It was a rhetorical question to which I wasn't expected to supply an answer; a silence followed.

"How would you like to meet Picasso?" he asked.

I said yes, I would very much, and it was arranged that we'd drive early the next morning to Vallauris, where Picasso was then working on his ceramics.

Thanks to André Verdet, Picasso accepted me, although I learned later that he was unforgiving toward anyone who might nibble at his time. He took André by the arm and led him to his studio. I followed. They stood chatting by the sculpture of a large and spiny goat with huge udders. There was a transvestite look about it, as if she was really a billy goat. I took a picture of it, and then asked Picasso to stand by himself next to the goat. I snapped—the Leica's first clicks. The day wore on, and unaware of my outrageous behavior, I requested that Picasso go and sit in a nearby field of high grasses, take with him pad and pencil, and draw. He did as told. The result was my first portrait, posed, directed, thought out.

We returned to Vallauris a couple of days later because my services were required as interpreter. Picasso had agreed

to meet an American collector at the café in the town square. We sat outdoors at a table covered with a paper tablecloth. In front of us, in the center of the square, stood the Picasso sculpture of a shepherd holding a lamb in his arms. The American collector, a man in his late forties, was visibly moved. Shortly after the usual preliminaries, the collector spoke of the way he had acquired the master's drawings and prints. I translated. While listening, Picasso pulled out a pencil and started making quick, nervous drawings on the paper table covering—artist and model, bulls, women. The collector was entranced. It was a moment he would never forget. Picasso, with a wave of the hand over the paper, quietly said, "It's yours."

Picasso was fiendishly intelligent and knew what would follow. "I'm overwhelmed," said the collector, "absolutely overwhelmed. Please, would you sign it?" Picasso signed it. "*Merde*," he said in his Spanish accent, "it's wrong, it disturbs the balance." He tore off the corner that bore his signature. He applied his name to another part of the tablecloth and repeated the maneuver again and again until all that was left of the paper was a fragment. "That's worth nothing," he said as he crunched it up and threw it away. For the collector, it must have been the Chinese torture known as the Thousand Cuts, in which the victim dies very slowly and painfully. "The idiot, he wanted to make sure that scrap of paper had an acquired value. Too bad for him!" said Picasso later.

Célia Bertin, a writer and a beautiful woman who lived in St. Paul de Vence, said, "Have you really photographed Picasso? I'll give you a letter so that you can visit Matisse in Nice."

Matisse's studio and apartment were in that part of Nice called Cimiez. A card pinned by a thumbtack to the door frame read HENRI MATISSE ARTISTE-PEINTRE. We rang. A woman led us to Matisse's bedroom, which was also his work place. Matisse was sitting in bed, drawing on a wooden tablet across his knees. Full-size sketches were traced directly on the walls, preparatory for the murals of a chapel in Vence, an inland town nearby. *Le Maître* had been warned of our arrival, and his kind, gentle face reflected by the way his smile greeted us his friendship with Célia Bertin.

Matisse was wheezing. I recognized the symptoms of asthma, an affliction that alas was also Natacha's. I had indeed noticed a cat lying quietly on the bed, hidden under the wooden tablet, but had kept quiet. Should I have suggested that the cat be moved out of the way? Unthinkable. Presently, Natacha too started wheezing, and bravely tried to hide it while I took pictures. We soon left. It was high time to remove her from the feline's presence.

The Leica never left me. I enjoyed taking snapshots of the white doves, of the twisting narrow streets of St. Paul, of the village women chatting around the fountain, of the cats sitting in windows, in brief of the obvious, the picturesque, the dubiously poetic. But somehow I also, by instinct rather than by deliberate thinking, recorded the postman delivering letters in the early morning, the Colombe's headwaiter and his daily strenuous physical training, the gravedigger's son who had become a self-taught sculptor, and the young girls in white looking like angels on their way to church for their First Communion. And of course, the writers, the painters, the potters, anyone who, as I'd always believed, was contributing to mankind's true call and salvation. When Braque turned up at the Colombe, I set him under an archway and snapped him. I'd now bagged Picasso, Matisse, and Braque. A good shoot.

Nevertheless, to Natacha's distress, I hadn't applied myself to thinking about the future. The present absorbed me. These were carefree, beautiful days. Mass tourism did not yet exist, cars were few, life was cheap, and the food of Provence simple and perfect. Tootling around the countryside in the MG—along the Mediterranean coast not yet buried under concrete, in the hills covered with olive groves and lavender—diverted my mind from the prospect of making a living in New York City. Natacha announced that she was returning

there with or without me. We'd been at the Colombe for over six weeks. I told her that I would stay on for another two and would then join her. I'd been invited to the inauguration of Matisse's chapel in Vence and didn't want to miss it. She left.

•

At the inauguration, while Monsieur le curé was delivering his homily, I took a walk around the chapel, camera in hand. I saw no one save for a man with a black Leica who approached me and asked what magazine I was working for. "None," I replied. At the time, if truth be told, I didn't know that magazines had photographers on their staff. "The way you stood, I thought you were a professional," said Mr. Black Leica, who then asked where I had my film processed. "At the drugstore in New York, close to where I live" (so far, I hadn't seen any of my photographs). The drugstore wasn't a good idea, I was told. I should try to spend a few days in Paris on my way back to New York and entrust my films to Pierre Gassman at Pictorial Service, 17 Rue de la Comète. "He will show you how to develop, how to crop, all kinds of things. And tell him I sent you."

"And what is your name?" I asked.

"Henri Cartier-Bresson."

And that's how I found out what I would do in life.

That chance meeting and the pictures of St. Paul de Vence opened the doors of the New York magazine world. Three years went by, and I'd turned into a successful photographer, when on assignment in Europe, on a night train from Paris to Lausanne, I found myself sharing a sleeping compartment with another man—Cartier-Bresson, still with his black Leica at his side. I introduced myself, asked him if he remembered our meeting at Matisse's chapel. Yes, he did. He looked at me quizzically. "Have you ever regretted that meeting?" he asked.

4

Alexei Brodovitch

When you saw him, it was hard to imagine that this stooped, fragile man in a buttoned-up grey suit was a Russian aristocrat who as a boy had met the Tsar weekly; as a young man attended the Corps des Pages; as a cavalry officer in the Hussars fought in the First World War, and later in the White Army against the Bolsheviks. Speaking in a voice barely audible, chain smoking mentholated cigarettes, he appeared so distant as to be forever beyond reach. He was the art director of *Harper's Bazaar*, an immensely talented graphic artist, an innovator and, as I first knew him, a teacher. Although he died in 1971, he is still a mythical figure among art directors, and his name a byword among photographers. Those who worked with him, or for him or under his guidance, often say, "I think of him almost every day."

When I started to attend Brodovitch's Thursday evening classes in Richard Avedon's studio in 1952, all I had to show were my few snapshots from St. Paul de Vence. About twenty men, rarely women, came to these workshops, all of them professional photographers with the exception of myself. I knew nothing.

The mention of technique was taboo. It was kitchen talk. All that mattered was the exercise of eye and brain to produce surprise, astonishment, and information. Information was the key word: what you already know is not information. Indeed information covered everything as long as it revealed something heretofore unknown or, more simply, unnoticed. Whether reportage, a cigarette advertisement, or a page of fashion, it had to fit the notion of information. "Look at thousands of photographs," he used to say, "and store them in memory. Later, when you see in viewfinder something reminding you of familiar picture, don't click shutter." Originality and surprise, that's what mattered. He was a hard master. At every session, we were given a task for the following week. If there was no time to accomplish it, we could bring magazine tear sheets, as long as they related to the problem at hand. Sometimes, the assignment could be deceptively simple: "Bring a photo you like." On one of these occasions, as he was turning over and discarding a pile of prints on the table, he stopped and held up the photograph of a nude seen from the back, the girl holding a rose in the crack of her ass. At the foot of the picture, the author of this oeuvre had added Gertrude Stein's hackneyed *"A rose is a rose is a rose."*

"Who did this?" asked Mr. Brodovitch. A hand went up. "Very vulgar," said Mr. B. with his heavy Russian accent. "Reminds me of wallpaper in cheap hotel in Lille, north of France." With "Children" as the week's assignment and without any prearrangement, we all went to the poorest sections of New York and shot Black and Puerto-Rican kids playing around garbage cans. All prints were peremptorily dismissed. "You all stupid. You all believe poor children more interesting than rich children. Anyway, Cartier-Bresson photographs of Spanish children already done before war and much better. You must think: I am art director of fashion magazine, have no use for this. Why nobody photograph Madame de Rham's dance school for rich children?" At another time, we were asked to produce a layout. Brodovitch knew the few pictures I had taken, and it was essential to produce some he hadn't seen. I chose to photograph New York bridges at night, a quick task with the subject right at hand.

Around midnight I was standing on the Williamsburg Bridge over the East River, the camera on a tripod directed at the moon, which was visible through the bridge girders, when a couple of men approached me. The first one asked what I was doing. "Shooting the moon," I said. The second wanted to know if I agreed with Cartier-Bresson's ideas. He introduced himself: "I'm John Cage, a composer, and this is my friend Richard Lippold, who's a sculptor." Pointing to a house at the Manhattan end of the bridge, Cage explained that members of the New York artistic and musical avant-garde were living there, that when I was done with the moon we should go back to his studio, he'd wake everyone up, and we'd have a party. The project "Bridges" was dropped in favor of the project "Avant-Garde." I took photographs over the next few days and clobbered them into a layout.

The following Thursday, Brodovitch gave his verdict: "Photos good, layout zero." He also requested that I present myself the following morning at his *Harper's Bazaar* office. Good news awaited me. He would publish "Avant-Garde" (which came out as "The Bosa Mansion," the Bosas being the building's owners who lived on the ground floor), and he'd give me enough work to open a studio. However, I would be *la bonne-à-tout-faire*, French for the cleaning lady who also shops, cooks, takes care of the children, and does the laundry. Irving Penn, he said, had been trained for still life, Richard Avedon for fashion; I was to engage in beauty, fashion, still life, reportage, portraits. Everything.

I opened my first studio above a sawmill on East 86th Street. By and large, I managed to acquit myself of my tasks, although the first fashion sitting was an ordeal. I had no experience of fashion photography, had never seen a fashion session either in studio or on location. Worse, I was not working with experienced models but with two young society girls, one wearing a Balenciaga, the other a Dior dress. Many hours were spent in the darkroom to produce ten acceptable prints. Brodovitch riffled through them and put two aside. "Just publishable," was all he said. I then made a fatal mistake. I said, "You have taken me on, and it's my first fashion assignment. Tell me where I went wrong." Brodovitch gave me his Siberian gulag stare. "When I look at Leonardo, I say I like. When I look at Stewart, I say I don't like. Good-day Mr. Stewart." It was a blow, but let's face it, I'd been compared to Leonardo da Vinci.

When Carmel Snow, the magazine's editor-in-chief, criticized a layout, she could not be addressed this way. Brodovitch would not oppose her but said yes and did nothing, never changed anything, and got away with it. Retreat and dig in were his tactics. His wife, Nina, was the other power in his life. She was a large woman who dominated him physically and psychologically. Alexei (as I was eventually permitted to call him) had ambivalent feelings about her, something I found out when they came for dinner at a summer house I'd rented in Springs, Long Island, close to theirs. No sooner had Nina laid eyes on my young son Nicolas, than she spat out "I hate children!" Brodovitch whispered to me, "Hell to live with such a woman." After dinner when a large urine stain spread through Nina's skirt as she was sitting in an armchair, another whisper: "Ah! Marvelous woman!" Russians . . .

Jack Dunbar, his assistant at *Bazaar*, and June, his wife, went to visit the Brodovitches at their organic farm in Chester County, Pennsylvania. A new bull had arrived, and Mr. B. wanted his guests to view it in its enclosure. Jack described a mythical animal of huge proportions, stomping at their approach. "Terrifying," he said. "We stopped at a respectable distance, but not Nina, who went ahead, vaulted over the enclosure and approached the bull, who stood motionless, watching her. She then crouched under it, took its testicles in her two hands, turned to her husband, and said 'That's balls, Brodovitch!'"

After Carmel Snow and Nina had died, his life turned into a tragic Russian story. He became an alcoholic and was sacked from *Harper's Bazaar* without a pension after twenty-four years of service.

His teaching career and his ancillary activities unraveled. Old students tried to help him financially. He retired to France, to Oppède-le-Vieux in the Luberon, near Avignon, where his brother George was an architect. At his request, in 1970, a year before his death, I went to see him, motoring down with my two assistants. We found a sunken old man, sitting outside at a table, listening to a small transistor radio and stroking a cat. He lived in a sort of troglodyte shelter, half cavern, half farmhouse, and slept on a camp bed under which were piled copies of *Portfolio*, a beautiful magazine for the graphic arts that he'd founded long ago and which had survived only briefly. He hardly spoke at first, but little by little became more voluble. I suspected he saw no one but his son Nikita who hovered barefoot in the vicinity. We carried Alexei to restaurants: he had broken a hip and moved with difficulty.

When I first abandoned advertising and then editorial assignments to concentrate on personal work—large black-and-white photographs of still lifes—I struggled with Alexei's ghost. I felt it hovering behind me; I heard it rebuking me. In no way could that work fit the ideal of information; nor was it destined to be printed in a magazine and the original print discarded into a wastepaper basket, as my old master occasionally used to advocate. Without doubt, he would have disapproved. He might have said, "What is use of this?" Now, I'm not so certain. After all, he'd once asked me, along with Irving Penn and Richard Avedon, to attend one of his workshops. He wanted to prove that he'd kept up with the times. We were shown the work of his star student: projected on a screen, we saw photographs of Picasso's black-and-white bullfight engravings shot through colored filters; and for a soundtrack, the fanfare of the corrida. Yes, Alexei had changed, and surely he must have seen my recent work in *Photo*, a French magazine that had given it the lead story. It was through the magazine that he'd got in touch with me, and therefore perhaps my qualms were misplaced. Or so I hope.

5

Music

Steinberg and Munch

It was going to be a long day: portraits of several New York conductors for *Harper's Bazaar*. I'd met some of them through my mother-in-law, a celebrated pianist, the only woman who had ever played with Toscanini.

The conductors had appointments and would come to my studio on East 73rd Street one by one. The background of grey seamless paper and the lighting were set up in advance. Technical considerations wouldn't interfere with directing my "sitters." Conductors, like most performers, have fat egos, as well as (but then who hasn't?) inner images of themselves that they wish to project. The photographer may decide to play up that secret image, or, on the contrary, attempt to reveal what he perceives to be the *persona* of whoever is in front of the camera.

The first to arrive was William Steinberg, who would later direct the Boston Symphony Orchestra. He was a rather small man with an unusually large nose and, unlike many of his colleagues, was modest and unassuming. To achieve a somewhat flattering rendition of my sitter required flat lighting and a frontal view. All went well, we got along, and William Steinberg left without having suffered too much.

Half an hour later, it was Charles Munch's turn. I think that Munch was retired by that time (he died five years later, in 1968), but he carried himself with that particular dash, a casual elegance found in the past among Paris boulevardiers, as the breed used to be called. It could be said of him that he was a "breezy character." As he walked toward the set he looked at me, raised his left eyebrow in an ironic way, and asked, "Who was your last patient?"

"William Steinberg."

"I see," said Munch, *"der Nosen Cavalier."*

Ania Dorfmann

My mother-in-law, Ania Dorfmann, who as a young girl had come from Odessa, was famous both for her interpretation of nineteenth-century piano pieces and for her malapropisms when she spoke English. She owned an apartment on Madison Avenue across the landing from her mother's, whom we called "Baba." The arrangement was perfect because Baba provided her daughter with all her meals. Ania had no use for her kitchen, and she turned it over to me when I first decided to take up photography. It was my first darkroom.

At the time, Ania was working on Schumann's *Papillons*. The piano was in the living room and highly audible in the darkroom. *Les Papillons* became my photographic *petite madeleine*: that piece invariably takes me back to the long and frustrating hours of my apprenticeship, more powerfully even than the flat smell of hypo, the chemical that fixes the print when it comes out of the developer.

The blessed day came when Ania moved from Schumann to Bach. This was more to my liking, and I congratulated her for varying her repertoire. "I am certain," she said, "that this will be a feather in my asset."

She was the *grande dame* of the Julliard School of Music, where in her studio she had two Steinways and a large oil portrait of Toscanini. My younger son Alex once went to meet her there for lunch at the cafeteria. Alex remarked that she had a surprising number of African-Americans (though the appellation wasn't in use then) attending her master class. "I am no racist," said Ania. "When a Negro kisses me, I am not revolted."

Invariably, a revolving door was "a revolting door."

The day came when Baba became too old to cook, so Ania, who had recovered her kitchen (by that time I had a studio, a darkroom, and an assistant), had to start fending for herself. Her knowledge of culinary art was not limited; it was nil. Baba gave her the necessary instructions for soft-boiled eggs. Ten minutes later, Ania was back in her mother's place.

"They're dancing in the water! What do I do?" she cried.

"Play them a Chopin waltz," said Baba.

Poulenc and Duval

Francis Poulenc came to be photographed on a very cold day. He was wearing a heavy, black coat and on his head a hat called a Homburg. He was a tall, imposing man and re-minded me of General de Gaulle. With him came his favor-ite *cantatrice*, his adored singer, Denise Duval. As usual, the background and the lights had been set and I'd asked my as-sistants to go round the corner and have a cup of coffee. The session, I thought, would best be conducted in French, and my little scenario would be more acceptable if no strangers were present.

I greeted Poulenc when he came in and he introduced me to Duval. I suggested he keep his hat and coat on and

stand in front of the background as if waiting to hear a young
woman who had asked for an audition. She would then sing
for him. The idea pleased them both. Denise Duval remained
at the back of the studio, pretending to be shy and playing
nervously with her gloves. Poulenc called her over, "Come
over, Mademoiselle, we are waiting for you."

Duval came forward, Poulenc lifted his hat to salute her,
and asked her what she intended to sing. It was *Les Mamelles*

de Tirésias, music by Poulenc himself, words by Guillaume Apollinaire.

Denise Duval looked up at Poulenc and started singing.

J'ai envie d'être soldat une deux une deux
Je veux faire la guerre—Tonnerre—et non pas faire des
    enfants
Non Monsieur mon mari vous ne me commanderez plus
Ce n'est pas parce que vous m'avez fait la cour dans le
    Connecticut
Que je dois vous faire la cuisine à Zanzibar.

Poulenc took up the lines.

Donnez-moi du lard je te dis donnez-moi du lard

and joined Duval for the next lines. He threw off his hat and took her in his arms. Together they sang,

Vous l'entendez il ne pense qu'à l'amour . . .*

And they kept on singing and hugging while I clicked away.

When the composer died in 1963, Denise Duval stopped singing. I was told that the only photograph of Francis Poulenc that she kept in her apartment was one of those I took on that cold day in New York.

---

* I want to be a soldier one two one two
  I want to make war—damn it—and not babies
  No, my good husband, you can't order me around anymore
  It's not because you wooed me in Connecticut
  That I've got to cook for you in Zanzibar

  Give me some lard, I tell you, give me some lard

  Listen to him, he only thinks about love . . .

Wanda Landowska

That "old Jewish woman crazy about music," as she used to say of herself, lived in Lakeville, Connecticut, when I went up to see her. She was indeed old and cranky, as well as domineering.

I was quietly ushered into the studio, a large living room furnished in a traditional half New England, half European way. Three women, friends and collaborators, hovered around Wanda Landowska. I told her I first wanted to listen to her play and hoped, when I started working, that she would not mind the sound of the camera as I clicked the shutter.

She sat down at the harpsichord, adjusted her long, black, frilly dress, rubbed her hands together, and started on a Bach partita. After a couple of minutes, head down, the fingers running on the keys, she muttered a word that I didn't catch. One of the three women reached for a small round tin of candies and took off the lid. Another woman, who wore fine white gloves bordered with lace, took hold of the tin and walked over to the harpsichord. Holding the box in her left hand, she seized a candy with the thumb and index of her right hand and popped it into Landowska's open mouth. The partita suffered not a whit. Shortly afterwards, another call came, and this time I understood it clearly, "Out bonbon!" The bonbon woman walked up to the harpsichord once more, placed her gloved hand under Landowska's mouth, and out came bonbon into her palm.

The light changed, and I needed to take a new meter reading. Landowska was still working on the Bach partita. I could see a slight movement of her cheeks as she sucked on another bonbon. Quietly, I moved toward her, trying to be unobtrusive, and brought the light meter up to her face. A hand approaching her mouth called for a Pavlovian reflex, and Landowska ejected the bonbon. It hit the light meter with a small click and fell on the floor. The partita came to a stop, we all laughed, and Wanda Landowska said, "Enough photos, please let's have tea."

6

A Day with Karen Blixen

Night had fallen. A candle was burning in every window to celebrate, as happens yearly, the Germans' departure from Denmark on 5 May 1945. The house, half-timbered and two stories high, topped by a steep gable, cut a sharp but dark silhouette against the night sky. Isak Dinesen's house, the Isak Dinesen who, when she is not writing, is known as Karen Blixen—Baroness Blixen. The house's name is Rungstedlund. It's midway between Elsinore and Copenhagen, close to the sound, in days past a relay for coach horses and an inn where, for a few years in the eighteenth century, it's most famous occupant was Johannes Ewald, Denmark's greatest poet.

Imagining the owner of the coffee plantation in Kenya; remembering her friends and neighbors, her lovers and servants; her relations with workers and their families; recalling her life with the animals she had tamed and the big game she had hunted—in brief, all that's told in her books seemed immensely distant from the small and aged lady I was introduced to. Yet, one impression came through and obliterated the diffidence and the weaknesses of the years: She was a *grande dame*, a woman imbued with a nobility of being that rested not so much on caste and education—often ineradica-

ble—but mainly on character, that mixture of inner compo-
sure, self-imposed rules, manners, and bearing.

Three women—friends, not servants—were present in the
house at all times. Furniture was eighteenth-century Danish,
but the sobriety of the interior was softened by the gossamer
cotton curtains that framed the windows and trailed on the
floor in random circular patterns. Here and there, but especially in the room where Karen Blixen worked, Masai shields,
spears, and masks hung on the walls.

Meals were formal, the silver and glasses the best, but Baroness Blixen ate slowly and sparingly. Sometimes, her meals
consisted of a small portion of caviar, which she took up from
her plate with a three-pronged gold fork. A spoon would have
done better, but no doubt a fork was more elegant.

Karen Blixen had agreed to have me photograph her at
the request of American *Vogue*. She'd said nothing concerning my presence in her house, but it was my guess that she
might entertain second thoughts about bending herself to a
photographer's whims for several days. I told her that, having seen her marvelous house and what she had done with
it, this photographic essay should be hers and not mine; that
her taste and her talent for storytelling should dictate the way
she wished to present the house where she was born, where
she lived, and which treasured the memories of her African
years. I asked her to accept me as her assistant: I would deal
with technical matters, and she would direct the photography. The proposition seemed to please her.

"Very well," she said, "we shall start with the great oak
tree under which I wish one day to be buried."

We walked over to the tree, which stood free and vigorous,
spreading its roots amid the spring flowers studding the lawn.
I set up the tripod with the Rolleiflex (a camera with a rel-
atively large ground-glass image), framed the shot, and took
the light readings. Obeying instructions, I walked over to the

tree while Karen Blixen stood at the camera and directed me. "You stand, please, ballet position number three, facing me." I took the stance.

"A flock of birds is flying above you from right to left. Lift your head and follow them with your eyes."

Checking the ground glass, she took one final look, left the camera, and moved to the tree. Her back to me, she stood squarely mimicking my stand, finally ordering me to go and take the shot.

So went the day, with more photographs both indoors and out. That evening, as we were having a glass of wine before sitting down to dinner, Baroness Blixen turned to me and, without a smile, announced that she'd had a good time, that she trusted me, and would I please return to my true profession, that of photographer.

7

Ladakh

Oracles

"I wish I could go to Tibet," said the American girl.

In the early 1980s, Tibet was an impossible tourist dream. My friend merely voiced a long-held belief that Tibet was Shangri-la, the place where spirit prevailed over matter, where strife and striving were unknown. The Tibetans held the antidote to the ills of the Western world. She'd surely forgotten, if she ever knew it, how James Hilton's best-seller, *Lost Horizon*, and Frank Capra's movie in 1937 had launched the Tibet myth. She was familiar with the books of Lobsang Rampa— flying monks, giant mummies from the time when Earth's gravity was weaker and men grew taller, surgical openings of the Third Eye, and other nonsense. Lobsang Rampa, if I remember rightly, turned out to be an English plumber's son and had never left the British Isles. I told the girl to forget it. Tibet was locked tight.

A day or so later I dropped in to see my Paris travel agent, and a modest leaflet scotch-taped to the wall caught my eye. It read Now you can go to Tibet! The leaflet referred to Ladakh, a high-altitude desert of the Trans-Himalayas, in the northwestern part of the Indian state of Jammu and Kashmir. A few restricted areas were open to foreigners. I booked two tickets to Srinagar in Kashmir, and called my friend to tell her that she was getting closer to her dream: Ladakh is known as "Little Tibet" because in many ways it's a miniature replica of Tibet itself.

I'd seen enough of the East to know that the serene doctrine of Buddhism didn't prevent its followers from engaging in the cruelty and the baseness prevalent in mankind, but in time I too shared the challenge that had exercised so many Westerners: to enter Tibet and see Lhasa. In the meantime, Little Tibet would have to do, but of this three-week journey in 1976 I will say only this: I resolved to return for a long stay.

•

By November 1981, after a six-month spell in Ladakh, I needed to renew my Indian visa. That required a flight to Srinagar, for only there could it be obtained. Winter had set in early in Kashmir, and return flights were temporarily cancelled. The weather held me prisoner. Flying into Ladakh is tricky and unpredictable: the plane must swoop down from the Zoji-la, the high pass over the mountains that separates Ladakh from Kashmir, slip through two or three defiles and land in Leh, the capital, with its primitive runway. The road is snow-bound eight months a year.

In olden days under the Raj, such was the attraction of a summerhouse on the shores of Srinagar's two lakes, that the sale of land to British residents was banned. Hence the houseboat, a legal substitute. Summer on the lakes is still a dreamy experience. Reclining in your shikara, the local punt, you drift among the lotus. You watch flights of bulbuls and of crested hoopoes, the Buddha bird, as they raid the floating gardens. Slim barges, laden with fruit and flowers, slowly slide by on their way to market. Beyond, your eyes rest on the jagged peaks of the Himalayas. But now icy winds blew down from the mountains, and joined the bone-chilling damp rising from the lakes. The "wily Kashmiris," as Kipling called them, slouched about wrapped in their brown cloaks, shivering figures of melancholy. To escape the town's dismal atmosphere, I retreated to a houseboat. But, snug tight inside my sleeping bag, I could feel the rats trotting on top of me, no doubt looking for an opening. I moved back into town.

There were no foreigners in Srinagar save for two Germans who, like me, were awaiting a flight to take them to Ladakh. Peter and Walter had come from the University of Bonn. Peter was in his twenties and studying Tibetan. Walter, "an old Tibet hand" as he labeled himself, had been taken prisoner by the British during the War and sent to work on a farm in Scotland. The experience, he maintained, had given him a permanent longing for oat biscuits and whiskey. Peter and Walter planned to spend the winter months in Ladakh and record the Gesar Saga, the Tibetan legend of Gesar, who liberated his people from the rule of demons. The saga may be recited only in winter and at night. As no one knows it anymore in its entirety, the plan was to tape it in discrete parts that would eventually be spliced together. With them was a Ladakhi scholar, Mr. Gergen, key to the project and its success. At last the weather cleared and we all left—the Germans, Mr. Gergen, and I. On that flight I found myself sitting next to a young Frenchman, Hughes Costa, who was making a survey of countries abutting on Tibet—Sikkim, Bhutan, Nepal, and Ladakh—for the CNRS, a prestigious scientific institute of the French state. I suggested that he stay in my usual billet in Leh, the schoolmaster's house. It was clean, and equally important, the owner and his wife catered to the Western mania for washing: when the temperature rose to zero degree Celsius I would ask my hosts for a bucket of tepid water, climb on the roof to catch the sun's warmth and have a wash.

At the time, Leh had a population of only three thousand people, one street called the Bazaar, and a maze of winding alleys. Its main feature was the king's palace, a downsized replica of the Potala in Lhasa, and above it, on the Peak of Victory, the Namgyal Tsemo monastery. The Ladakhis wore *chubas*, heavy cloaks dyed in rhubarb juice, Buddhists and Moslems lived in harmony, and the sun shone three hundred days a year. It was almost Shangri-La.

Mr. Gergen and the two Germans moved to a house at the edge of town. We met nightly for dinner. We also attended festivals, the great winter attraction of the local population. The festivals take place in the inner courtyard of monasteries with the monks assuming all of the roles, the gods as well as the devils. Ceremonies and rituals owe not so much to Buddhism as to Bön, in Tibetan countries the cult that prevailed before the arrival of Buddhism in the seventh century of our era. Central to its beliefs is the existence of archaic furies and demonic forces, perennial threats that must be guarded against. Bön priests are shamans: they exorcise, predict the future, fall into trances and commune with the spirits that inhabit the land, the rivers, the trees, the mountains. Equally shamanistic is the cult of necromancy and divination. Bön has largely merged with Buddhism, but it survives, still known as "the religion of the people." Its importance is such that in Lhasa the ranking figure immediately after the Dalai Lama was the State Oracle. So far, none of the festivals we'd attended had featured oracles, though I'd witnessed the performance of a *lhamo*, a female oracle and healer, who lived in the village of Sabu, some fifteen miles from Leh.

Once a week, people flock to her little house to be healed. The room is always crowded. Her son, a sergeant in the

Ladakh Scouts, the local regiment, acts as beadle and keeps order. I had asked him if I could take photographs of his mother. He transmitted the request and she questioned me sharply: Did I know anything about Buddhism? Did it have meaning for me? I answered yes to both questions and was given permission to take pictures as long as I promised to keep the film in "a clean place."

The *lhamo* intones her chant in a thin, metallic voice. She examines a few grains of barley she's thrown onto a small drum, covers her head with a black cloth, falls into a trance, and exorcises the devils with high-pitched curses and incantations. When she comes out of her trance, she deals with patients. One by one, they come up to her and bare the ailing part of the body—breasts, belly, neck, limbs. The *lhamo*, like a bird of prey, seizes the ailing part in her teeth and sucks out the illness. After a while, she pulls away, turns sideways and vomits a stream of black mud into a brass bowl.

The evening preceding the festival in Stok, Mr. Gergen warned us that for the first time we'd be meeting the oracles. They were dangerous, they cast spells, and they hated foreigners, particularly those carrying cameras. "You, John," he said, "with all your equipment, you should be very careful."

He probably noticed a fleeting suspicion on my face.

"Don't be such a *pukkah sahib*, a proper, old-fashioned Englishman," he said sternly. "Last year an oracle chopped off an Australian's hand. They carry swords."

•

The festival, the *cham*, was nearly over. The villagers, jam-packed in the monastery's inner courtyard, were now restive: the oracles were about to appear. Shouts and the sounds of struggle erupted from the main building. I hid my two cameras beneath my oversize parka and went in to investigate. A dozen monks were attempting both to restrain and to dress two young men who were in a state of manic agitation. Screams filled the hall. Although, in the true sense of the word, the scene was demonic, it was more reminiscent of a lunatic asylum, the attempt to force two inmates into straightjackets. Most often, local monks take on the role of oracle, but this time in Stok two young and strapping villagers had been chosen and trained for the function. They'd been led out of their cells and readied to appear. I left the hall and took up position in the crowd behind a big and hefty sergeant of the Ladakh Scouts. I'd enrolled him as my assistant—to hide behind his bulk and use his shoulder as a tripod.

The two oracles came out of the main hall as if expelled from a gun. Lance in one hand, sword in the other, barefoot and screaming, they ran down the crest of a narrow wall and jumped among the terrified villagers who retreated in confusion. They climbed onto a wide ledge. One of them bared his arm and started slashing himself with his sword. The other appeared to be cutting off his tongue. Blood flowed, people screamed. I clicked away until I needed to reload.

"Run! They've seen you! Get away!" my sergeant-assistant whispered in a hoarse, urgent voice. I heard the wail of the oracles behind me, and escaped, pushing my way through the crowd. A ladder was propped along a wall. It led to a roof, and I scrambled up. The villagers on the roof shouted at me to get off. I raced around the roof and found a stairway at the rear of the building. By the time I was back in the crowd, the oracles had resumed their self-mutilation.

When the *cham* was over, I met up with Hughes Costa. He looked bruised and disheveled: unable to catch me, the oracles had turned on him. We drove back to Leh in a sullen mood, but there was one more ordeal: The two Germans and Mr. Gergen had given a lift to a Ladakhi we all knew and admired, a young man of immense strength and endurance, who for no apparent reason, turned on Mr. Gergen and started beating him up.

The Stok festival was to resume on the following day, but I came down with stomach problems, and Mr. Gergen needed to rest after his rough handling. We both stayed behind while the others returned to Stok. I urged Hughes Costa to take care, more specifically not to shove his lens under people's noses, as he often did, but to use discretion and a long lens. Mr. Gergen and I met at a teahouse. I wanted to hear more about the oracles.

"All this business of drawing blood, just a magic trick," he said. "Anyway, they're all filled with booze. Just booze . . ." Mr. Gergen was a Christian. His father, converted by the Moravian missionaries of Leh, had translated the Gospels into Ladakhi. Clearly, shamanism had been excluded from Mr. Gergen's beliefs.

Our friends returned from Stok with bad news. Hughes had once more been set upon while the oracles were busy foretelling the future, and had now taken to his bed. A bunch of villagers had kicked and punched him, his nose was battered, and he was badly shaken. Later, he joined us and we heard more details: he had feared for his life when the oracles closed in on him but strangely this time they didn't touch him, they just contemplated the villagers' work. Amazingly, he said, not a scar, not a trace of their self-mutilation was visible.

I left Ladakh in early spring, a couple of months later. Hughes had entrusted me with twenty rolls of film to hand over for processing to his father in Paris. I flew back to London and mailed the film. I'd been commissioned to produce a book on Ladakh, and later I went over to Paris to show my publishers the photographs I'd taken that winter. Pasted on walls, I saw yellow stickers advertising lectures and slide shows about *Les pays limitrophes du Tibet*—countries abutting Tibet. The lecturer's name was Henri Costa. I wondered why Hughes had changed his name to Henri. I called him but no one answered the phone. Presumably he hadn't yet returned.

I dialed his father's number, and a woman answered. I asked to speak to Hughes. There was a short silence, and then in a strangled voice, she said, "You had better speak to his father."

"Hughes died two days ago in Delhi," said his father. "I would have called you in London to let you know. We don't have any more information, except that it was hepatitis."

Hughes had been only twenty-four. He was a gifted young man, intent and eager, nervous and questing, but he had never fitted into the quiet, almost meditative round of existence that prevails among the Ladakhis. It is said of the young who die early that the gods are jealous. In Bön terms, he had not propitiated the gods, but set himself apart from them.

His father asked if I could shed any light on this awful loss. I had nothing to say.

"But who is Henri Costa?" I asked.

"It's beyond any understanding," said Hughes's father. "It's a mystery—almost the same name, the same research. I have no idea who it might be . . ."

I called Peter in Bonn.

"Peter," I said, "I've heard terrible news."

"Yes, isn't awful? Poor Mr. Gergen."

"What do you mean?"

"Don't you know? Mr. Gergen is dead. We found him, Walter and I, in his room. He died while he was shaving. We were in Drass at the time." Drass is a village known for being the coldest place in Ladakh.

"Do you think the cold killed him?" I asked.

"*Ach*, no. He was just dead."

I asked Peter if he was in good shape. His German accent was more marked than I remembered it.

"We brought Mr. Gergen's body back to Leh. In a truck, you know, an old machine. You remember the road along the Indus near Chilling? Perhaps the brakes failed or perhaps the direction. Anyway, the truck left the road and fell on the riverbank. I broke my arm and three ribs."

"And Walter?"

"Walter wasn't hurt. But he had that awful cough. Even when you left, yes? Then it got worse, and the doctor in Leh could do nothing, so I took him to the military hospital. One day, I visited him. 'I am dying,' he said. I knew he was right. But then he also said, 'Only the *lhamo* of Sabu can save me.' I went to see her, and you know, she did something she never does: she came to Leh. We brought Walter back to the house where we were living, and she did the sucking. Two days later, Walter was much better."

I broke the news about Hughes. There was a long silence and I thought the communication had been cut. It hadn't. "John, what happened to you?" Peter asked.

A couple of days before this conversation I'd gone to see my publishers. About sixty slides of the winter's sojourn had been slotted in a Kodak carousel and secured by a screwed-down plastic lid. The carousel was then fitted inside its cardboard box, and as it was raining, I slipped the box into a heavy white plastic bag. In the rue de la Chaise, close to the Boulevard Saint-Germain, two schoolboys on the run slammed into me. I staggered, and the white bag flew out of my hands. I saw it rise slowly above my head and reach its apogee, at which point it hovered before beginning its descent. It tipped. The bag opened. The box came out, and so did the carousel. An extraordinary thing then occurred: the plastic lid unscrewed, and a shower of slides floated down into the gutter, where a stream of rainwater was gushing away down into the Paris sewers. I uttered no word of anger, let out no sound of anguish, but knelt down to block the slides floating down the gutter and stuff them in the plastic bag that had landed at my feet. Three or four were lost. I returned to the apartment where I was staying, and dropped the slides into the sink. I went to a hardware store to buy clothes pins and a ball of string. On my return to the apartment, I hung the slides to dry. I also tried to make sense of the event.

Time had slowed down as if I'd been watching a slow motion film shot at forty-eight frames per second instead of the usual twenty-four. Simultaneously, my inner state had been affected so that instinctual reactions, whether words or gestures, never occurred, or occurred so slowly that I controlled them. I'd stopped being the helpless witness of events within my own references, but had slotted myself into another time frame.

Of the five of us in Leh, I got off most lightly. I didn't lose my life, and my health wasn't affected. Moreover, all the slides were saved. I found near duplicates for the few that had disappeared into the sewers. The book, however, has never happened. Over the years, four different publishers have tried to bring it out. For a number of reasons, they all failed. I'm the only one aware of the true reason.

The Nubra Valley

I was filled with doubts; anyone would have been. How could Véronique, an Indian masseuse who worked out of a modest house in a West London neighborhood known as Shepherd's Bush, possibly give me access to Madame Indira Gandhi, prime minister of India, daughter of Pandit Nehru, and leader of the second most populous nation of the globe? Yet that's exactly what happened.

My friend J., a talented sculptor and *femme du monde*, was a follower of Véronique. (You can't say a client, a customer, or even a patient; it would miss the point.) Like many women of her tribe, twice a month, more if needed, J. drove to Shepherd's Bush. Twenty-four hours after a visit, you knew: she glowed, and a waft of exotic unguents emanated from her. The treatments were holistic—mind as well as body. The cost was that of a top-rate psychoanalyst.

"I wish you weren't so cynical," said J. "Be nice to Véronique. I'm sure she can help you. Anyway, she's beautiful. Offer to do a portrait. And you'll take photographs of the house. Don't forget the bathtub."

Véronique was indeed beautiful in that fusion of femininity and statuesque stance occasionally found in Indian women. The "atelier" as she called it, was just what you would expect: couches, massage tables, cabinets of Ayurvedic substances . . . and the bathtub. It stood in the middle of the room, an old-fashioned zinc tub encased in a polished mahogany box. A mild electric current could be circulated through the zinc lining. I got out a camera and started recording the various stages of the treatment, J. acting as my model. The tub was filled with warm water. J. undressed without any qualms and entered the water. I clicked away. We laughed. It was all very jolly.

At last we got down to business. I explained my request. Only specific areas of Ladakh, where I proposed to spend the best part of a year, were accessible to Westerners. In the course of my stay, I wanted to travel along the Nubra River, north of Leh. It was the caravans' route from Xinjiang to Ladakh (Xinjiang is the Han appellation of Chinese Turkestan). The Nubra Valley, however, was strictly out of bounds. Hostile neighbors were found on three sides: China, on the northern and eastern borders; Pakistan on the western. The area was the preserve of the Indian armed forces all the way to the Karakoram Pass, the frontier with Chinese Turkestan. Eminent scholars, Tibetologists, some of them personal friends of Mrs. Gandhi, had applied for permission. Everyone had been turned down.

"Of course, Mrs. Gandhi is very sad," said Véronique.

I asked why.

"Because I'm here and she's in Delhi."

I kept my thoughts to myself.

"You must write a letter," continued Véronique, "and mail it to me. Just explain what you want. I know what to put on the envelope for her to get it directly."

•

Two months later, in early spring, I was having dinner with the Assistant District Commissioner in Leh.

"Forget about the Nubra," he admonished me. "I can go there. Ladakhis can go there, but unless you're Army, better forget about it. An American tried it some time ago. He was discovered, thrown in jail to teach him a lesson, and then evicted from India." A few days later I received a letter from J. Veronique had been advised by Mrs. Gandhi that she could not let me travel to the Nubra Valley. The hotels were "not up to standard."

I flew back to London in September to assemble the equipment required to face the winter months when the mercury can go down to thirty degrees Celsius below zero. Most important was a sleeping bag bearing a label that ensured survival down to minus thirty-five. Within twenty-four hours of my arrival in London, where I was staying with my sister, I received a communication from the high commissioner for India—Mrs. Gandhi's approval—and two more the following day, specifying the conditions of the journey.

In Leh, the impossible happened: I became an instant folk hero. Tibetologists are a jealous lot, and inevitably I heard envious comments. "Why him?" they said. "I've been here longer than he has, and I speak Ladakhi." Others claimed that they were more qualified than I was. All of it was true. Local officials, however, had not been advised. The only resort was a

quick trip to Srinagar in the hope that the Kashmiris had ne-
glected to forward Delhi's signal to their Ladakhi colleagues.

When I faced him, the minister for the Department of Internal Affairs, State of Jammu and Kashmir, dismissed my
request with the contempt proper to civil servants the world
over, until I produced the documents from the high commissioner. The minister, using both thumbs, simultaneously
punched two old-fashioned electric knobs sitting on his desk.
Two men entered from opposite doors. "Find the Delhi file
regarding travel to the Nubra." Within three minutes the file
was produced and I received my permit.

A "liaison officer" from the police department and a guide
were detailed as escort. Both these young men's families lived
in the Nubra Valley, and would be helpful. No jeep driver,
however, was willing to take us to Deskit, the main village
of the region, whence the serious part of the journey would
start. All feared the season's first snow and a problematical
return to Leh. Eventually a jeep owner who had family in
Deskit reluctantly agreed to take us for an extravagant sum.

•

The jeep rumbled along the Central Asian Trade Route, no
more than a wide path at the edge of stubbly fields where
giant Himalayan crows were pecking at the grains left over
from the gleanings. The wind blew away the chaff. The
clouds were low. Twice my papers were checked by Indian
troops living in tents by the side of the route. They were shivering in the cold, and their faces were gray.

The road climbed relentlessly. Toward evening, we came
to a small house, half mud, half stone. There lived a man
whose pale eyes were glazed with the same resigned look visible in his sheep. I was invited to spend the night in a stone
hut absolutely bare save for a *charpoy*, the traditional Indian
bed of string and wood. Hanging on a hook above it was the

pallid carcass of a sheep. My two companions stretched out in the jeep.

The following day we crossed the Khardung-la, one of the two highest passes that the caravans had to negotiate. The other, the Karakoram, is slighter higher. "The Karakoram is the father," was the saying, "and the Khardung-la is the son. The father is huge and old, but the son is young and terrible." There was in fact no need to use the pass any longer. The Indian Army had built a road that skirted the foot of the mountain and crossed a glacier further on. I wanted to experience caravan travel, and to the incomprehension of my two companions, I insisted on walking up to the pass.

We climbed slowly. The air was thin. There was a rasp in my lungs, and my heart was pumping hard, but I was free of altitude sickness. My companions, true Ladakhis, were at ease. It took four hours to reach the pass at 18,380 feet.

We looked north. Below us, two small lakes—one as black as polished basalt, the other dark emerald—and the glacier. Bleached strips of cotton flew from willow branches stuck in a pile of stones, a Bön latho. Of the Buddhist stupa, only a crumbling base remained. Under our feet, on the dry and icy ground, ancient signs of the caravans: fragments of harness, a discarded boot, frayed ropes. And bones, bleached by the sun and the wind. Bones of sheep, camels, horses. The last caravan had crossed the pass in 1950 when the Chinese Communists had put a stop to "the capitalist vermin" leaving the country to trade abroad. The Turki caravans, particularly those on the haj, were told, "Don't bother with a guide, just follow the bones." Pilgrims, soldiers, merchants, bandits, and monks had crossed this pass, and there we stood, the three of us, facing the mountains to the north, arms extended above our heads, faces up to the sky, and cried out the incantation of the Buddhist traveler: SO, SO, SO! LA GYALO! DE THAMCHE PHAM! HO! *The gods conquer! The devils are defeated!*

•

We reached Deskit at the confluence of the Shyok and Nubra Rivers. Lower than Leh, Deskit had the lush intimacy of an English village in spite of snow-covered mountains on both sides of the Nubra. Wheat, rather than barley, grew in miniature fields. Wood pigeons and magpies nested in walnut and apple trees. Hollyhocks grew wild around summer pavilions. At the crossing of wall-lined paths, wind- and water-driven prayer wheels purred without cease. Deskit was my dream place: no greedy Kashmiri merchants; no monks offering fake objects of the cult; no touts to lead you where you had no wish to go. Yet the inhabitants deplored the ban on tourism. They wanted to be consumers; they craved the goods of the modern world. They said, "No, that would not change our ways of living," when I described the greed and the changes that were visible in Leh, but to no avail.

I was staying with my guide's family, and as I was unpacking my gear a man came with orders to follow him to the police station. A radio message had been received from Leh concerning the arrival of an Englishman in Deskit. The communication had been cut off in the middle, and it was assumed that the Englishman, like the American in the past, was to be arrested and sent back. When I produced my papers I could see disappointment on the face of the police chief.

•

Rosy was the owner of four Bactrian camels, descended from or left over from the time when the caravans traveled from Yarkand, in Chinese Turkestan, and from Lhasa in Tibet. The Yarkand caravan took one month to reach Leh. "The worst journey in the world," wrote Sven Hedin, the Swedish explorer, in the 1900s. Deskit offered the ultimate chance to replace the pack animals that had perished on the journey,

or sheep that would be slaughtered on the way. Following the tradition, I took on Rosy and four of his double-humped camels.

Mrs. Gandhi's authorization allowed me to go no further than the last hamlet before the Karakoram Pass. It turned out to be an easy journey, mostly along the river, occasionally crossing it, which were the only times I climbed on one of the camels. We stayed in monasteries or in peasant houses, and once in a go-down, as warehouses used to be called, where the British had stored opium that was being illegally introduced into China (a trade that led to the Opium Wars in 1839), while the caravans on their return journeys from China brought *bhang*, or hashish. The last *bhang-munshi*, the last keeper of the go-down, had been my guide's grandfather.

After crossing the Khardung-la, I saw no more bones, no more traces of the past, except for large stone tombs along the path, tombs of the Muslim haji on their way to Mecca, of the caravan merchants, and of their horsemen.

We reached Panamik, a village of two hundred inhabitants. Six miles beyond, a hamlet marked the limit of my journey. Sonam Tashi, a friend who in Leh doubled as a post-office employee and guide for trekkers, was the owner of one of its three houses. I wrote him a note to say that at noon the following day he'd find me across the ford from the hamlet. A villager delivered it that night. That hamlet had been the caravans' last human dwellings before facing another two weeks of high glaciers, vast deserts, traitorous ledges, and fatal precipices, until they crossed the Karakoram Pass.

We left Rosy and his camels in Panamik and had a pleasant three-hour walk to the ford. Sonam Tashi and two other men were waiting for us. They wore their best *chuba*, and their wonderful Ladakhi hats, which are worn at a fetching angle on the side of the head. They'd also brought a horse with fine Tibetan rugs under its wooden saddle so that I wouldn't have to get my feet wet.

Sonam Tashi introduced me to his two brothers. I climbed on the horse and was led up to the house where Tashi's wife greeted me. I met the three children, as well as a youngish man about the house. We all sat down to lunch. Tashi's wife brought the dishes. Tashi took care of pouring the *chang*, the barley beer.

The family structure was a polyandric ménage, both more complicated and more beguiling than it appeared. Although polyandry—one woman with several husbands—is banned by Indian law, it was still quietly practiced in remote areas. Tibetans love traveling in their mountains and are often away from home. A woman marrying a man becomes a "semi-wife" to his younger brothers as long as they're not monks. In return for tilling the land and taking care of the farm, the brothers have access to the wife's bed when the legal husband is away. Children's biological fathers are known roughly by working out who was home nine months before their births. The situation is further complicated by the presence of a lover. As soon as she gets married, the wife may choose a lover who is generally assigned a number of tasks in and out of the house. On dismissal, the lover is entitled to a reward—whether money or cattle—depending on the duration of his stay. The young man about the house was, of course, the lover.

On our way back from Tashi's hamlet, a man hailed us from across the river: Was I English or American? English, shouted back my guide. "Then would he know the name of the American president?" "Reagan," I shouted back. "Well, he's been assassinated. I heard it on the radio," said the man across the river. At the next village, I met the *goba*, the most important landowner and effective headman. I questioned him about Reagan's assassination. "I know nothing about that," he said, "but President Sadat of Egypt was killed. You know, anything that happens outside the Nubra Valley, happens automatically in America."

Caravans

Here is the story I heard from a very old man one night when we were staying in his son's house:

"When I was young, the caravans were every boy's dream. An adventure. But after three months of travel, these boys came back home thinking that trading in the bazaar, sitting in a cubicle no larger than a donkey's stall, wasn't such a bad life.

"It was the hajis who suffered most. It was a whole year before they returned home. It was a sight: old men and women, sometimes children, carried in boxes, one on each side of the horse. They wanted us to sell them food and mounts. But my father said 'Never try to cheat them. Don't sell them one-eyed mules, or lame horses, or stubborn donkeys.' They were poor, the hajis, and that's all they could afford. Many per-

ished on the way. They lost their way in snowstorms. They died of cold, even of hunger. They were attacked by Kanjut bandits and carried off to be sold as slaves.

"Caravan stories are mostly about death and suffering, not so much about money. My own father once told me a strange thing. He was at Skyangpo-che, about ten days from here, and he'd gone off a short distance from the campsite to gather bushes for the fire, when he found the body of a woman. She was curled up at the foot of a rock, a baby in her arms. My father said she could have been sleeping, with her long black hair spread out on the snow, and a blanket around her shoulders. The wolves had not touched her. 'I could not leave her there under the sky, but when I tried to move her, she and the baby turned into white dust. All that was left of them was hair, bones, and bits of clothing.' So spoke my father.

"I was only six when I heard this, and I made up stories. I used to try and imagine why she went off to die with her baby—stories that frightened me as I went to sleep."

•

Back in London, I went to see Véronique. How had she managed to get me permission, after all?

"Simple enough," she said. "Last summer, as you know, was the royal wedding, Prince Charles and Diana. Mrs. Gandhi sent her son Rajiv to represent her. I had lunch with him and reminded him to tell his mother to do something about John Stewart."

Yes, simple enough.

8

Astral Stories

In spite of the many years I've spent in France I am still unsure how I should respond to the question "What sign are you?" My instinctive reaction is to say "smoked salmon," but it's a tricky answer if you don't want to offend, and it has to be delivered with a smile and an air of self-deprecation. Invariably, a woman has asked the question. Men seem to shy away from astrology. If they believe in it, they don't talk about it. Even François Mitterrand, that cold-blooded Cartesian scholar and classicist, regularly consulted two astrologers while he was president. Germaine Teissier was his favorite. (Her thesis, which earned her a doctorate at the Sorbonne, was entitled "Epistemological situation of astrology across the ambivalence of fascination/rejection in post-modern societies.")

For a while, in Paris in the 1980s, I was occasionally asked to dinners attended by a coterie of high-flown civil servants, literary figures, and opera lovers. Among them was an attractive woman who worked for a French publisher: she ran the section devoted to books on psychology. Her name was Joëlle de Gravelaine, and I was told—by then we had met a few times—that she was one of the most prominent astrologers in France. I dismissed the information, yet when I next met her I got her to talk about the subject. Of everything she said I only recall why, in spite of her reputation, she no longer practiced astrology. Working out horoscopes, she explained, was too time consuming, although she made an exception and still did it for three people: Jonas Salk, the inventor of the polio vaccine, who then lived in Los Angeles; a physicist at CERN, the European nuclear research center in Geneva; and a psychoanalyst in Paris. Whenever he took on a new patient, he claimed, her readings saved several sessions normally devoted to preliminary investigations.

As we were leaving the dinner party, at a moment when the others were out of hearing, I asked her if she would read my horoscope. I was feeling silly and self-conscious, but Joëlle said with a smile, "I've told you I don't do it anymore, but we've met a few times, you're an interesting man, and if you can give me the hour of your birth, I will."

I applied considerable pressure on my mother whom I telephoned in London to get the needed information. She guessed immediately why I wanted it ("John, you must be out of your mind!"), but reluctantly she admitted, "Before teatime." I relayed the news to Joëlle. "It's not good enough," she said, "but as I know you morphologically I may be able to determine the exact hour of your birth. If so, I'll call you." This made no sense at all, but I decided to go through with the experiment, and some ten days later Joëlle called: I was born at 5:15 P.M., she announced, and asked me to come over to her apartment the following Saturday.

After lunch in the company of her son and a friend of his, she dismissed the two young men and deployed on the dining-room table three sheets of paper bearing circles and notations. She started to describe what she claimed were crucial events of my life, most of them accompanied by psychological footnotes. It took about twenty minutes, after which she asked for my comments.

I tried to present a detached attitude, but I was deeply troubled by her insights. In no possible way could she have come by her knowledge of my childhood and adolescence. I pointed out some intriguing errors, or rather slip-ups. She had said, for instance, that when I was four years old my father had been very ill. My parents had, in fact, separated for a year, and my father had gone to live abroad. "I saw that he was away from the family," explained Joëlle, "and I took it for granted that he was in hospital." It was an astonishing performance but for one fact—not a word had been said about my wife and my family, yet I had been married for over fifteen years.

"Of little importance," said Joëlle.

"How can you say that?"

"You have always needed passion in your relations with women, and you never had it with your wife."

She was right. I got married for all the good reasons but without a whiff of passion, although I'd experienced that agonizing and wonderful state before my marriage. My wife must have suffered from it. She was Russian, and hence was addicted to the psychodrama (a facsimile of passion) without which Slavic people don't really feel alive. When angry, she'd accused me of being "a cold English fish."

That, however, was not the end of the matter, for Joëlle, who did not even know my ex-wife's name or possess the slightest information about her, started to give me a profile, her looks, her talents, her poor state of health, her weaknesses, and her strengths—none of which had anything to do with astral readings, the configuration of planets, the place, date, and time of my birth. There was no doubt about it: Joëlle was reading my mind. She was a medium. No other possibility existed. Here was a talent that I rated far higher than astrology. For almost two hours, I had been sitting next to a sorcerer.

9

Pochoir

It might have been the roster of artists, both French and foreign, who were living and working in Paris between the two wars: Foujita, van Dongen, Utrillo, Kisling, Derain, Picasso, Marie Laurencin . . . Gouache, watercolors, ink washes, oil on paper, came out of the plan-chest drawers. All reproductions. Not an original among them. All utterly perfect copies turned out by means of pochoir and turned out in the atelier of two brothers, Pierre and André Jacomet.

Pochoir is French for "stencil." Basically, it works by selecting the different colors of an original piece of art, and then cutting templates in thin sheets of zinc to the precise shape of each color. Each stencil is placed in registration over the final support—a faint sepia of the original—and the color is applied to its respective zinc stencil by means of a blunt brush not unlike an old fashioned shaving-brush. It's one of the means to produce exact reproductions, although the process demands time, extreme precision, and much experience.

The story is told of a panic moment in the gallery of Heinz Berggruen, a celebrated Paris dealer, when Jacomet prints of Matisse watercolors got mixed up with the originals. There was no way of telling the originals from the reproductions until someone thought of looking at the back of the prints. Pencil smudges marked the originals.

In Paris, in the 1970s, the two Jacomet brothers still ran a pochoir production inherited from their father, who had refined the process by linking it with collotype printing. Their place of business in the Montrouge suburb of Paris had the look of an Atget photograph. The first time I went to visit the brothers, the clouds hung low and the cobblestones in the courtyard glistened under a thin drizzle. The half-timbered workshops were wrapped in the grayness associated with the small manufacturing plants of the Industrial Revolution. In this scene, a tumbrel and horse would have fitted better than the Renault van parked there.

I had brought with me five large photographic prints of haystacks, shot in the Vexin country, halfway between Paris and Normandy. The prints had been toned sepia and, with a light hand, I'd colored them with acrylic paint. The plan was to produce a hundred portfolios each containing the five views.

The brothers showed me around the plant. Collotype presses occupied the ground floor. Collotype is a method of printing images without a screen. It uses a heavy sheet of glass coated with a light-sensitive gelatin able to register a photographic image; a chemical process turns the gelatin and its image into a continuous tone plate similar to a con- ventional lithographic stone; the prints come out of a flat- bed press. On the day of my visit, they were monochrome views of Cairo in the eighteenth century. The presses them- selves were reminiscent of an age when man's inventiveness was visible in machines that carried their own special beauty: machines that took me back to my childhood, when I vis- ited my grandfather's factories in North London; and also to my favorite toy, a German Märklin steam engine of gleaming brass and polished steel.

On the top floor, seated at individual tables, rows of men and women were laying down pochoirs over the collotype prints and applying colors by means of a tool similar to a shaving-brush. They were coloring the Cairo prints, each print requiring the application of eighty pochoirs. The registration was impeccable, no sign of smudging was perceptible and the sharpness was perfect. So was the silence, save for the dull tap-tap sound of brushes applied to paper.

We retired to the office to discuss my own project, which required only two pochoirs. I noticed three modestly framed, medium-sized paintings hanging on the wall—gouache or watercolor, it was hard to tell. Nor could I identify the artist.

"I see what you're looking at," said the older of the Jacomets, "and I'll tell you a story. Chagall once turned up here with ten paintings he'd made in Provence. No goat in the sky playing the violin, you understand, but typical Provençal stuff—landscapes, olive groves, views through a window, and the like—what you see on the wall. He wanted an edition of twenty. We went to work, and after four or five months we sent him a note saying that when he next came to Paris he should come and see our tests, and if he approved of them, sign *a bon à tirer*, the order to start printing the series. He came one afternoon, inspected carefully what we'd done, and abruptly turned around on his chair. 'You must stop all this,' he said. 'No one will ever be able to tell the original from your reproductions.' And he left.

"Some six months later, Monsieur Chagall turns up here unannounced, a brown paper parcel under his arm. He unwraps it. It's a pile of heavy white paper manufactured specially for him by the Arjomari-Prioux people. You know them; they have this famous paper mill in the Auvergne. Chagall then holds up a sheet against the light. 'Here, have a look,' he tells me. Well, you know what the watermark read? It read '*Ceci est une reproduction*,' signed 'Marc Chagall.'

"Chagall smiled and said, 'Now you can go to work.' But that's not the end of the story, because he kept a few sheets of that watermark paper and used them for some of his original gouaches and watercolors. It's possible to own an original Chagall certified by the master to be a reproduction."

"What do you think went through his head?" I asked.

"Simple enough—his way to confuse the critics and the experts. Simply '*pour emmerder le monde*,' just a way to get his own back on the riffraff of the art world."

10

Cigarettes

Ballooning

Once a year, I was sent to different parts of the world to shoot a Lucky Strike cigarette advertising campaign. Invariably, the man holding or smoking "the product" was a fine representative of the male species. "A Man's Cigarette," read the copy. These assignments necessarily involved violent or dangerous situations where nerve, stamina, and courage were key—for the performers, not for me of course. I was merely recording their exploits.

One of the ads was to show intrepid balloonists crossing the Alps. We were taking advantage of a rally featuring a dozen participants who had enrolled for this challenge. The meet took place in Mürren, a village in the Bernese Oberland of Switzerland, and a great jumping-off platform that looks straight down into a deep, green valley, two thousand feet below.

I arrived in Mürren a few days before the start of the event and booked myself at a hotel with a terrace facing a great Alpine trio: the Mönch, the Eiger, and the Jungfrau with its glacier. An old English lady was spending all her waking hours

A LUCKY

LUCKY STRIKE
IT'S TOASTED

CIGARETTES

MADE IN U.S.A.

on the terrace. She'd set up an old-fashioned brass telescope mounted on a wooden tripod, and occasionally she would get up and peer through the eyepiece. The telescope never moved; it was directed at the base of the Jungfrau glacier. I asked her the reason for her vigil. She explained that in the summer of 1932, she and her young husband had come here on their honeymoon. The husband went out for a day's climb on the Jungfrau glacier, mentioning that he would cross it at its narrowest point. He was never seen again. The crevasses were probed. Some are very deep, and there's no doubt that he fell to his death in one of them. As everyone knows, glaciers are never still because of the vast mass of ice slipping on the rock bed and other factors. They move forward at a very slow pace. The old lady had consulted the local authorities who had calculated that her late husband's frozen body was likely to appear within a month, if indeed the initial premises of fifty years ago were correct.

•

In preparation for my assignment, I had chartered a small plane, a high-wing Cessna, from which I could follow the race with my camera trained on the nacelle of the balloon where the occupants would be busy smoking Luckies while drifting over the snowy peaks. On the morning of the race, we took off from a tiny airfield in the valley, climbed high until we looked down on Mürren and the deflated balloons being readied to fill with helium and start on their adventure. There was a feeling of inaction about the place, but we had no radio communication with the base and could do nothing but keep track visually of what was going on below. After an hour of this—a boring and rather sick-making hour of incessant circling—when not a single balloon had managed to leave the flowered pastures of Mürren, the pilot said, "To hell with them. Let's go and have a look at the Spaniards."

He banked the plane in the direction of the Eiger, a massive and irregular pyramid, thirteen thousand feet high, with a worldwide and terrifying reputation. Its north face is steep, the weather changes violently, and ice can form rapidly. Many have perished on the face since the first escalade in 1858. The pilot skirted the aircraft close to the mountain and pointed out "the Spaniards," two bodies swinging gently at the end of ropes, half way down from the top. This was in May, and the bodies had been swinging since the previous October. A few crows flew about them, out of curiosity, I would imagine. There would not be much left to peck.

The Spaniards had started their climb from Kleine Scheidegg, the village at the foot of the north face. I know nothing about their skill as mountaineers or about their experience or their equipment. But their girlfriends had come with them to watch the climb. The weather was fine, and they were well on their way when they were overtaken by a party of Japanese who were proceeding up the face with greater ease and at a faster pace. Two hours later, however, the Japanese were on their way down. Their radio had announced a cloud bank that might turn to rain, with the danger of ice formation. They invited the Spaniards to join them for the return to base. The offer was turned down: the girlfriends were surely watching through field glasses, and they could not abandon the climb and lose face. They perished. The first party to go up the north face after my aerial visit cut the ropes. The bodies fell to the foot of the mountain and were given a proper burial.

But this was Switzerland, and a special detail could not be omitted from the story when I heard it: The Spaniards had been wearing automatic watches, on which the spring is constantly wound by the movement of the wrist. When the bodies were recovered, the watches were still in good shape and keeping time. The swinging of the bodies had kept them going.

Filming

I'm again at Kleine Scheidegg, but this time with a group, two representatives from the Philip Morris Tobacco Company in Lausanne, the art director of their advertising agency, my assistant, and three Swiss mountain guides. We're sitting on the terrace of the local inn, having coffee and beers. The guides have been engaged for a still photograph commissioned by Philip Morris: roped up, they are to climb a steep ice cliff on the Jungfrau, and light up when they reach the peak, which my assistant and I would, of course, arrive at by an easier route.

All had gone well, although the Philip Morris people lost their nerve halfway up and turned back. But now we were all assembled together, and the time had come, I believed, to propose a scheme I had in mind, namely to film the ascent of the Eiger's north face. It had never been done. My idea was to have a helicopter deposit a diesel winch with drum and cable on the summit, a cable long enough to reach the Eiger's base. The winch would haul up the cameraman and enable him to film the climbers. Necessarily, it had to be a *direttissimo* ascent. I put the scheme to the guides. There ensued a passionate discussion in Schwizerdutch, of which I understood just enough to feel optimistic. Finally, in English, they said yes, it can be done and we'll do it. Then came the question of budget. We calculated a rough figure, and the Philip Morris people said no problem.

There were, however, logistical and technical problems to overcome. A friend who knew Chris Bonington, a famous English mountaineer, suggested I approach him to head the expedition. "I'd better tell you," said Bonington on the phone, "that it's just been done by Yorkshire Television in Leeds." He told me whom I should speak to.

The producer of the documentary gave me the story's broad outlines: One morning, "two men with an idea" had presented themselves at Yorkshire Television. One was a plumber, the other was unemployed. They'd read accounts of the Eiger's north face, and they proposed to climb it and make a film. Had they any experience of mountains? they were asked. None. Did they know anything about filming? Nothing. Did they realize that any number of experienced people had lost their lives on the north face? They did.

They were taken on, a contract was signed, and they were sent for a week to some craggy hills in Yorkshire to acquire a rudimentary knowledge of rock climbing and its basic paraphernalia. They were also taught how to use basic eight-millimeter cameras.

Later, I heard details of the expedition: the way the "stars" had made a nuisance of themselves, the initial attempts that had to be aborted, and the actual climb in three days instead of the usual one or two. Finally, the two men had turned out a usable film—and they had survived.

The producer flew down to Lausanne with the documentary blown up to thirty-five millimeters. The major executives of Philip Morris gathered in the projection theater. The lights came down, and the Eiger comes into view—a splendid and frightening sight. This is followed by footage of the base camp, treated as if it is an expedition up Everest.

Then comes the actual climb. We see the two men on the lower slopes, slowly and hesitatingly ascending, roping themselves up, finding toe holds, gripping rocks, resting, filming, until at day's end it's time to stop and prepare for the first night on the face. There's no question, of course, of lying down, but they find two ledges, close to one another, where at least they can squat. They make themselves fast to the rock, ensuring that they will not fall off when they go to sleep. From their backpacks, they extract dried foods, and they drink cold tea from their water bottles. So far life is good, they're on the way, and the cameras are working. It's now time for a smoke. They get out their cigarettes and light up. There's hardly any wind, and a thin plume of blue smoke goes gently trailing away from the north face of the Eiger. The executives of Philip Morris all stood up. The applause was tremendous.

Yorkshire Television sold the film, and I got a story to tell.

Wild Horses

Another year, another Lucky Strike trip. I'm to photograph cowboys rounding up wild horses, and arrangements have been made in New York by the advertising agency. In Helena (capital city of Montana, population about twenty thousand), we're to make a deal with a powerful man, owner of several ranches. His name, somehow, has been erased from my memory, although "Bill Harrison" rings a bell, and that will have to do.

It was around eight in the evening when we checked in to a motel in Helena and called Mr. H. He was still at his desk and told us to come over, so the client representative, the art director, and I drove out to his office. It is almost unnecessary to describe the building: it was the Old West you've seen time and again in Westerns. No horses, but pick-up trucks parked in front of a three-storied colonnaded wooden building. The hall itself was sunk in darkness as we made our way to the elevator and its dim yellow light. An old cowboy with only one boot—a wooden peg peeked out of the left trouser leg—was in charge. He'd also lost his right eye, covered over by a black patch, and two fingers were missing from the hand that worked the hydraulic elevator. We rumbled past the first floor and heard a hymn being sung. "Fuckin' believers, have to stay up late for them every fuckin' night," said the old cowboy. As we all piled out at the top, he gave me a wink from his one working eye.

Harrison's office was huge, occupying the whole floor. Three or four naked bulbs of the 40-watt variety hung from the wooden ceiling, but above Mr. H.'s desk there was a bulb of a slightly higher wattage. It could be turned on and off by means of a short chain. With its rolltop desks and ledgers piled high on baize-covered tables, the place again gave me the feeling of déjà-vu—the old movie sets. Bill Harrison, tall, handsome, in his fifties, dark blue rumpled suit, stood up to greet us. We were invited to install ourselves in front of his desk, and he sat himself down in his swivel armchair, but then made a gesture indicating there was something to be attended to. He stood up once more to grab the chain above the desk and turned off the light. The scene was now far more *scuro* than *chiaro*, yet visible on the desk itself was a framed photograph of a young man raising his right arm, swastika on sleeve, in the Nazi salute. The picture carried a handwritten dedication: "To my friend Bill Harrison, George Lincoln Rockwell." The young man with the swastika was the head of the American Nazi Party. We held our comments for later.

We explained what we were looking for: a lead picture showing a pack of wild horses driven by mounted cowboys smoking Luckies. Among his different ranches, said Mr. H., he had just the one "that would fit the bill." For five hundred dollars, cash. The money was handed over, we shook hands, and were given instructions how to get to the place.

The ranch induced a sense of desolation. A dim grayness prevailed over the rundown buildings, the rutted trails deep in mud, the bare trees, the broken fences, and the sagging barbed wire. It was late March, and winter lingered. Dirty snow patches dissolved slowly under the drizzle, while cold and damp seeped into clothes. The breeze brought the reek of death: Mr. H. had worked out that during the winter months when cattle remained outdoors, he saved money by allowing a number to die rather than giving them the fodder to survive the cold. Not all the bloated carcasses had been hauled away. Their sight and stench added to the lugubrious feeling we all shared, thinking of the days ahead.

A dozen cowhands were housed in a long hut with a corrugated tin roof. Like everything else, it was derelict, but then so were its occupants. Each had at one time appeared before the local magistrate for some offense or other. They'd been given the choice of either a prison sentence or working for Harrison. The head cowboy was small, gnarled, bandy-legged, and incredibly tough. He was a Brooklyn Jew, hence he was addressed simply as "Brooklyn." These men must have received some pay, but I never knew how much. They were a sorry looking lot, who survived on a diet of beans, sow-belly, bread, margarine, and coffee. That was the extent of the menu, but there was no limit to how much they could consume.

The wild horses that roamed on Harrison's land were ungainly-looking and hairy. Occasionally there was a roundup when they were lassoed and corralled, some to be broken and used as mounts, others to be shot for dog food. Brooklyn had received instructions from his boss, and he asked me to explain what I wanted. Ideally, I told him, I needed to record a stampede of at least half a dozen horses from a low angle and frontally—meaning the horses running straight at the camera—with two or three outriders, cigarettes in their mouths. Short of placing a camera on the ground and working it by remote control, I could not imagine how it could be done.

"Trust me," said Brooklyn. We drove out in a jeep to select the spot where I wanted to shoot the stampede. That told him how the herd should be driven. He ordered a hole to be dug, deep enough for me stand in, but leaving head and arms above ground. Brooklyn assured me that the horses would not trample me. He offered a demonstration with a couple of his mounts. I remarked that it would not be terribly convincing because they were, after all, trained horses. Finally, I had to believe him and go through with his proposal. It all worked out as he said it would. The wild horses, at full gallop and terrified by the outriders screaming at them and twirling their lassoes, made straight for my hole, sidestepping it at the last moment. I got the shots and downed a whiskey when it was over.

Mrs. Harrison and her niece came to spend a weekend at the ranch. They went riding in the rain, and the niece's horse got tangled up on barbed wire, tore its belly open, and had to be put down. We were invited to the "Big House" to have tea. This was a large mansion built in the mid-nineteenth century during the Gold Rush (there were more millionaires in Helena at the time than anywhere else in America), and not much had changed in the gloomy interior with its massive furniture, heavy drapes, and a spittoon in every room.

The job done, we left the ranch, and shook hands with everyone. They'd all been very helpful and I was still alive, no bones crushed or broken. The cook, a large, pasty-faced man with a big belly, had a special request: "I been here come twelve years now," he said, "and got me no single one postcard from nobody. You be going back to the big wide world now. Send me a postcard, will you? You write 'To Jake, the Cook, at Mister Harrison, Helena, Montana.'"

•

I flew back to New York, and over lunch with one of the *Vogue* editors, I gave an account of the Montana adventure.

"There's something else to add to your story," she said. "A couple of years back, a somewhat nondescript woman stood in front of the window of Van Cleef and Arpels, the jewelers at Fifth and Fifty-seventh. The pièce de résistance in the window was a diamond-and-ruby necklace that had once belonged to the Impératrice Eugénie, consort of Napoleon III. The woman was staring at it, and then entered the store. Now, you know what the salesmen of these great jewelers, like Cartier, Harry Winston, and others are like—inveterate snobs—and the junior salesman at Van Cleef got a nod from the senior one, indicating that he was to take care of the frumpy new arrival. It was rather early in the day, Louis Arpels had just sat down at his desk—his office was just behind the main room—and the door was open. He overheard Junior describing the necklace, and his instinct told him that this was for real, so he left his desk and took over. The lady was your Mrs. Harrison. She bought it! I don't know how much for, but it must have been a hefty price. Anyway, she gave the name of her bank manager in New York, and everything was OK. There was plenty in the account.

"A year goes by and Mrs. Harrison turns up again in New York. She drops in to see Louis Arpels. Maybe she buys herself a bauble or two, and Louis says to her, 'Mrs. Harrison, you tell me you leave Helena once a year, only to go to New York. Please, I'd like to know, what do you need these great jewels for?'

"Mrs. H. says, 'My husband is a very rich man. He gives me all the money I need. But in all our married life, I have never received so much as a flower, never mind a jewel. Now, you see, I'm a member of the Ladies Bridge Club of Helena, and we meet every Thursday night. My friends put on their jewels, so I too . . .'"

11

Litmus Tests

Whenever I face someone for the first time, I'm instantly attracted or repelled—not in an obvious, powerful way, but in an obscure, subterranean fashion. Is it conditioning, instinct, or pheromones? Perhaps a little of all three. But if there's uncertainty, I ask myself: "Could I spend ten days with him or her, in a lifeboat?" It's one of my several litmus tests. I have my favorites, in effect two stories. Some see them as nonsense, while others think I'm pulling their leg. And then, of course, some get the point of stories that in turn deal with two crucial questions: the idea of God and the respect for life.

When Isaac Bashevis Singer won the Nobel Prize for Literature in 1978, I happened to hear him interviewed on BBC radio. He was asked to speak about his idea of God. Singer replied that he had none in particular.

"But there's not a single one of your novels or your short stories," said the BBC man, "where God, in some form or another, fails to appear. He generally comes in through the front door, occasionally through the service entrance, but he's always there."

"Are you addressing the writer," asked Singer, "or me as an individual? They're two different people."

The interviewer would not take that as a proper answer.

"Very well," said Singer, "I'll tell you a story about a South Sea Islander, a man with the I.Q. of genius. The island where he lived, however, was still at the Bronze Age level. One day, like most days, he went out fishing when a typhoon destroyed his outrigger canoe, although he managed to swim ashore to a desert island. After a few days, as he was walking along the beach looking for food, he saw something shining in the sand. He picked it up: a watch still in working order. The fisherman had never seen anything remotely like it. But, as I told you, he was extremely intelligent, so in a couple of days he understood how the movement of the hands related to the course of the sun in the sky.

"'Now,' he thought, 'let's try and see how this organism functions.' He managed to open the watchcase, and within a

few days (remember his genius I.Q.) he figured out the work-ings—the spring that could be wound, the escape mecha-nism, the cogs, and the wheels. In another week, he'd put it together again.

"'This is really wonderful,' he thought, 'but if you con-sider evolution and nature's incessant creation over billions of years, it's no wonder that eventually something like this should have come up.'"

For his seventh birthday, Roman Vishniac received a mi-croscope from his grandmother. He hooked it up to a camera and photographed the leg of a cockroach enlarged 150 times. This was in Moscow. Later, inevitably, he became a biologist and an expert in microphotography.

In 1918, his family moved to Berlin, where Vishniac pur-sued a successful academic and scientific career. The Nazis came to power, and he had an intuition concerning the fate of European Jews, and especially those of Central Europe. From 1935 to 1939 he made incessant journeys, recording Jew-ish life in towns and villages—religious schools, horse deal-ers, shopkeepers, cobblers, and rabbis. Occasionally he was arrested as a spy, but he'd taken the precaution of also pho-tographing monuments. That was the purpose of his work, he'd explain, and there happened to be Jews around them. Of the 16,000 photographs he took, he managed to save 2,000 when, after a short period of internment in France in 1940, he moved to America.

In New York, he resumed his career as a biologist spe-cializing in microphotography. His laboratory was on Central Park South, and that's where a *New Yorker* magazine writer came one morning to interview him for a "Profile." Vishniac told him that the New York Health Department had asked him to investigate the microbiology of the Pond in Central

Park and that he had to go down and gather a mud sample. They went off together, and Vishniac filled several test tubes.

In the course of a long day, the slides were prepared, photographed, and the film developed. When all was done, Vishniac told the writer that he had to go back to the Pond. "Do you need to pick up some more mud?" asked the writer.

"No," answered Vishniac, "I must return the mud to the Pond. It contains living organisms."

12

A Paris Childhood

My governess surely had a lover. Not that I knew it or even imagined it at the time (I must have been five or six years old), but now I'm certain that was the reason for our repeated visits to Luna Park.

Luna Park, on the western edge of Paris, by the Bois de Boulogne, was a fun fair open all year round. Whenever we went there, my governess and I, it was straight to the same attraction stand whose manager was probably her *chéri*. What I got to look at wasn't of much interest to a small boy—a *petit-bourgeois* bedroom, open on the spectator's side. A young woman lying on her back occupied the bed. You didn't see much of her, because the bed covers were pulled up to her chin and she was reading a book. A string net, moreover, was stretched where the bedroom's fourth wall would have been, the spectators on one side, the girl on the other.

One franc bought you six wooden balls. A circular target with a red center hung immediately above the net. Whenever anyone managed to hit it, a wondrous thing happened: the bed tipped sideways, the girl fell out, and rolled on the floor, stark naked. She'd then get up, push the bed back in place, rearrange the sheets, and tuck herself in, ready for the next successful throw. The first time I witnessed this scene, I was dumbstruck: My mother used to take me to museums where I'd seen innumerable paintings of nymphs and goddesses with smooth, pink mounds of Venus. The truth was at last revealed, and I concluded that paintings were inventions and deceits.

My sexual education might have been furthered some years later when I was thirteen or fourteen. I was not as proficient in Latin as was expected of me, and a priest, an *abbé*, was found to coach me. He lived on the Rue de la Harpe, off the Place Saint Michel in the Quartier Latin. Nowadays, the street has been turned over to tourists in search of cheap exotic foods, mainly Greek and Turkish. But in the 1930s, it was typical of the dark and narrow streets of the neighborhood, where working-class people, low-grade government employees, and small shopkeepers commingled with the whores standing on the pavement, waiting for customers. The journey from home to the Rue de la Harpe, across the Seine, and into the mysterious Left Bank was as adventurous as an expedition to the Zambezi River and Darkest Africa. Home was the 16th Arrondissement with parks, greenery, wide streets, and fine buildings, the lair of the upper- and middle-bourgeoisie, proper, decent, and right-wing. I rode the bus, on the rear platform open to the wind, the sun, and the sights and sounds of the city.

Monsieur l'Abbé lived on the third floor of a small apartment house. The main room had books piled on floor and tables. It was somber and dingy. Monsieur l'Abbé smelled of dead mice—a flat, dusty odor, not as pungent as that of organic decay. I observed slyly his stained and faded cassock in an attempt to discover its source, but opted for the likelihood of a mouse dead long ago whose dusty remains were hidden somewhere among the books.

As I left my Latin master, the whores smiled at me: "*Et bien, mon petit,*" they would say, "did Monsieur l'Abbé teach

you what you wanted to know? Come upstairs, we'll teach you other things." Torn between dread and curiosity, I never went upstairs. Anyway, I thought my pocket money would have been laughed at, and Rue de la Harpe was adventure enough.

13

Château Lafite Rothschild

My luncheon companion was slim, smart, and well turned out in the basic black dress obligatory at French *Vogue* where she was the feature editor. She had pleasant news: American *Vogue* wanted a full feature on Château Lafite, the great Bordeaux vineyards belonging to the Rothschilds, and I'd been chosen as the photographer. Two weeks would be ample. I would live in the Château, and of course, wife and friends could stay with me.

My closest friends, George and his wife Lucy, flew in from New York, and Natacha, my wife (who lived with the children in a Swiss village where I joined them on weekends) came by train. So did I, from Paris where I had my studio.

The château's interior was pure Napoleon III, massive furniture, heavy drapes, a cloying opulence, a surfeit of dark-red plush, and grapes—images of grapes, repetitive, ubiquitous, inescapable, appearing on such unlikely artifacts as tooth glasses in the bathrooms.

We lived in Rothschild style. The bedroom allotted to Natacha and me had an exceptional feature—two fireplaces, one on each side of the twin beds, his and hers. Every meal was accompanied by a *millésime* Château Lafite, and if a white,

Château d'Yquem. The linen was the finest, the glasses Baccarat, the silver ancient and bearing the family's coat of arms, the five arrows. The food was delicious, all of it originating in the château kitchens from local produce. Moreover, the great vintners of the region, knowing I was there for *Vogue*, invited us to sumptuous dinners. Our digestive systems were getting an unusual workout.

I photographed the vineyards turning red; the splendid *chai*, the low and dark building where hundreds of barrels were lined up; the interior of the château; and below the château itself, the Barons' Private Reserve, where the oldest bottles, dating back to 1795, rested in the cool penumbra. After the French debacle in 1940, a German colonel arrived at Lafite with the intention of making it his headquarters. The Rothschilds had left, and the *maître de chai*, who in normal times is the estate's supervisor, took the colonel on a tour, ending up with the Private Reserve.

"This," he said, "is the greatest and oldest wine museum in the world. The Barons' own reserve. Colonel, I hope you will agree with me, there's only one German worthy of the contents of this cellar."

The colonel was in agreement. The reference no doubt applied to him.

"Glad, you think as I do," said the *maître de chai*. "I'm sure Marshall Göring will appreciate this. You and your staff can take whatever you wish, except of course from the private cellar, which must be made safe. I suggest you have a sentry stand at the door day and night."

By the war's end, not a bottle was missing. The story doesn't tell whether Hermann Göring knew about the cellar, but the *maître de chai* received the Legion of Honor.

The job done, I returned to Paris by train (everyone had left the château a few days before me), and at lunch in the

restaurant car I ordered a beer. It was cold, thirst quenching, a beautiful gold. Simple delights. The films were processed and sent to American *Vogue*. Alex Liberman, the art director, called to say they were "wonderful."

A month or so later, I had to go to New York. *Vogue*'s editor-in-chief had just changed. Diana Vreeland, my old boss at *Harper's Bazaar*, had replaced Mrs. Chase, and Mrs. Vreeland asked me out to lunch. No sooner had we been seated at our table than she put it to me, "I want you to be honest: Do you think Lafite is for us?"

I said no, the magazine's interest was not winemaking but the château itself. And the château was a Second Empire relic in no way appealing to our current taste.

"I'm so glad," said Mrs. Vreeland. "I was about to tell you, we're not going to publish it, so we'll have a pleasant lunch, you and I. When we get back to the office, you can pick up your slides at the art department and offer them to another magazine. If you don't get what we were prepared to pay you, we'll make up the difference."

Lunch over, I gathered my photographs and went straight away to the editorial offices of *Esquire* which bought the story. A problem remained. Elie de Rothschild, responsible for Lafite, had to be advised. I hit a wall. No one wanted to be the bearer of the news, neither Alex Liberman, nor Mrs. Vreeland, nor anyone I knew at French *Vogue*. I've always shied away from lawyers, lawsuits, and law courts, and I didn't fancy a legal summons from the Rothschilds. The problem was solved when I attended the opening party for the Banque Lambert's new building in Brussels. Baron Elie was there, I was introduced to him, explained the situation, and was given the green light.

Back in Paris, I learned the reason behind my assignment. A keen rivalry existed between Château Lafite and Château Mouton, the latter belonging to Baron Elie's cousin, Baron Philippe. Château Mouton was not "Grand Cru," the highest reward for excellence, although it reached that status in 1973. Lafite advertised in *Vogue*, Mouton did not. Yet Mouton received editorial space and Lafite never did. The reason was Pauline Potter, an American married to Baron Philippe, a woman who combined taste, imagination, and talent. Dinners never took place in the dining room, but in the gardens, in the *chai*, in the kitchens. She also imposed her views on the château's furnishings. All this proved to be irresistible material for the magazine. Finally Lafite complained: Why don't we ever appear in the editorial pages?

The photographs were published in *Esquire*, yet every Christmas I received a case of Château Lafite Rothschild. A satisfactory ending.

•

My marriage was unraveling. I still commuted from Paris to our Swiss village for long weekends to be with my family. On one particular Friday, I arrived at the chalet, and after greeting Natacha who was having tea with a friend, I went to the kitchen to get ice for a drink. I noticed an empty bottle of Château Lafite standing on the kitchen counter. I asked the cook what she was doing with that wine. *"Du boeuf bourguignon, Monsieur."*

"And who gave you that bottle?"

"Madame."

Natacha was allergic to alcohol. Wine talk bored her more than any other topic. Lafite for beef bourguignon was her way of opening hostilities. It was also the final spur I needed to go for a divorce. That bottle was the straw that broke the camel's back, although the French expression in this case would be more apt: *la goutte qui fait déborder le vase,* one more drop and the vase overflows.

Addicts

Dinner at the residence of the French Embassy in Bang-kok. The talk is about my next project, "The hidden side of Bangkok." Someone suggests a Buddhist monastery a hun-dred kilometers north of the capital where drug addicts go to be cured, with generally a few Westerners among them as well. The abbot, it appears, is an ex-Thai police captain. Prob-ably worth a follow-up. Up to this point I've come across only two subjects: an ancient opium den now turned into a Chi-nese brothel, and an underground canal, a *khlong*, used as a warehouse by criminals.

The long and narrow corridors of the brothel were lined with cubicles, doors open until "action time." What you saw was a wooden platform with a Chinese lying on his back, reading a newspaper and smoking. Occasionally he clapped his hands. Three girls then appeared at the door, one was selected and the door was shut. No more than five minutes later the girl let herself out.

As for the *khlong*, like most, it had been covered over with concrete to become a street. But it still could be navigated in a shallow punt, and below the street an extraordinary array of goods, stolen or smuggled, rested on wide platforms running along the side. The most surprising item I saw was a single-engine Cessna still in its crate.

Three members of the French Embassy came with me on the trip to the monastery, along with an American friend who spoke Thai and worked for the Peace Corps. On arrival, however, we were greeted by a Thai woman who presented herself as the interpreter. She'd been a successful business-woman in New York, and on her return to her native country had decided to further the welfare of this monastery rather than resume a business career. She explained that the abbot had resigned from the police after discovering that his colleagues supplied drugs to "clean" prison inmates as a means of acquiring new clients.

It was April, and the pre-monsoon heat was on us. The addicts had been sent home, and the monks too were about to move off to the cool of the hills.

The abbot was seated on a slightly elevated platform, in the traditional crossed-knee, lotus position. I sat in a similar way, on the floor, facing him. The treatment, he explained, consisted of two stages, each of a week's duration. The first aimed at eliminating the toxic substance. Daily, the patient was administered a green soup that made him vomit; he also sweated off the poison in the sauna. The second stage was concerned with his mind—meditation combined with talks and private encounters with the monks. Finally, a vow was made to the Buddha never to return to the bad old ways. The results were encouraging. In effect they were phenom-enal, 75 percent success for those who had undergone the cure, 15 percent failure. Of the remaining 10 percent there was no news. The success, explained the abbot, applied to the Buddhists for whom breaking a vow might have disas-trous consequences for their next incarnation. The West-erners' results were not as encouraging. They were asked to

address their oath to a Superior Being, and it didn't work very well.

Like many heavy smokers, I'd stopped several times—with the help of hypnosis, acupuncture, and tobacco substitutes—always failing after a period of days, or at the most, weeks. I now wanted to know if tobacco addicts ever presented themselves for treatment. "People like you?" asked the monk. I wondered whether he possessed a secret power; or perhaps he'd got a whiff of my body odor. A tobacco cure, I learned, generally required the two stages, but over a shorter period. Was I willing; was I interested? the monk asked. I answered yes. "Shall we do it now?" was the next question, and I felt uneasy, wondering how my French friends would react to what they'd surely call Asiatic mumbo-jumbo. My answer was evasive. The abbot rebuked me, "Don't give me a child's answer." I agreed to go through with it then and there. "For you," said the monk, "no green soup."

As for Buddhism, he needed to know whether I knew anything about the religion, and if so, could I address a vow invoking the Buddha. My answer being positive, I was instructed to repeat three times the abbot's words, pronounced in Pali.

"You've sworn never to smoke anymore," said the lady interpreter when it was all over. "You never will want to," rejoined the abbot. He might have detected a doubtful expression on my face. "Well, you might this evening when you have a drink, and tomorrow after breakfast. I will give you a mantra."

He wrote it on what looked to be a thin sheet of cigarette paper. "Pronounce it when you get the urge. Learn it by heart and then swallow it."

I bowed to him, hands before my face, and gave an offering for the monastery. "Now go to the sauna," ordered the abbot.

The French Embassy people said, "Are you aware of that man's power? We all felt it." We went to the saunas, one for men, the other for women. A young Frenchman joined me. "Along with you I took the vow silently," he said. We threw our cigarette packs into the fire, I my Kents, he his Gitanes.

Back in Bangkok, before dinner and after breakfast, just as the abbot had foreseen, I felt the urge. I said my mantra. The urge left me. A day later, I swallowed the little sheet of paper. That was the end, no withdrawal symptoms, no substitutes, no anguish, and I've never wanted a cigarette since that day.

There may be several explanations for what happened in that short hour, but to eliminate one possible speculation I must make it clear that although I have the highest regard for Buddhism, the doctrine of reincarnation gives me a lot of trouble.

15

Mother and Son

D r. Schermann was a graphologist, an expert in revealing character through handwriting. He lived in Vienna and had an international reputation. Appointments to consult him were made well in advance of his visits to the major capitals of Europe.

When I was a boy my family was living in Paris. For a while we had a cook of Hungarian origin, and I'd acquired a liking for goulash. Every morning before leaving for school, I would go and kiss my mother, who was still in bed. Then it was the cook's turn to come and discuss menus. On the day when, unknown to me, my mother had booked an appointment with Dr. Schermann, then passing through Paris, I asked, "Could we have some goulash today?"

At dinner that evening my mother admitted that she had torn a page from one of my school notebooks. When she showed it to Dr. Schermann, the world-renowned graphologist looked at it and murmured *"Er liebt gulasch!"*—he likes goulash. In the course of that session, I never heard if anything more incisive was ever revealed about my mother's only son.

That was not the only occasion when thought transmission, or whatever you wish to call it, occurred between my

mother and me. It happened as the result of a scandalous episode at the beginning of the war, an episode which bestowed on me a "reputation." It was Sunday morning, we were in barracks, and the previous evening I'd had far too much to drink. I was in bed, half dazed, when I heard the bugle calling for church parade. Clearly, I was in no way fit for compulsory Sunday worship, and I dozed off for a few minutes. By the time I returned to full consciousness, the barrack room was empty; everyone had left. I rushed out in my pajamas, mounted my ridiculous little blue Austin 7, which dated back to 1928, and drove to the parade square, right down the lines of 332 Company, Royal Engineers, 300 men lined up in ranks of threes. I pulled up in front of the company commander, Major Willis. I dismounted, stood smartly, saluted, and announced, "Sir, I regret to say I am pissed and can't attend church parade!" I then got into the car and drove back to bed.

Shortly after I got out of jail (three days and a month's deprivation of leave), I received a letter from my mother. "Dear John," it read, "I feel something awful happened to you on Sunday morning . . ."

16

Eugène

This is one more story about a servant and his master. As in the ancient tales, the poor are good and the rich are bad. It was told to me by my father, who knew the selfish master whom we shall call Antoine Steinberg, although this is not quite his real name.

Antoine Steinberg was a bachelor, a man of impeccable taste, a great antiques dealer, who was indefatigable in his search for the perfect ormolu or the rarest boulle, and whose eye never failed to detect the flaw, the glued piece, the fake. Only by appointment was it possible to visit his gallery on the Quai de Conti, on the Left Bank in Paris. Few people had seen the private rooms of his apartment except for what the French call *la réception*—drawing room, dining room, library—but all had met his Japanese manservant, Eugène.

Of course, Eugène was not the name he'd been given at birth. That was Watanabé. His master, however, whose secret mentor was Proust's Baron de Charlus, genuinely believed that France had reached the peak of cultural achievement, and he felt that, regardless of his own German-Jewish origins of three generations ago, he had a duty to help maintain the purity of the language, source and nourishment of all things French. Hence Watanabé became Eugène, and the name was chosen because Antoine Steinberg (A.S.) in late spring generally went to rusticate in Biarritz for a short month, and Biarritz had been the favorite seaside retreat of Impératrice Eugénie, Napoleon III's consort.

Watanabé, a.k.a. Eugène, incarnated the samurai's loyalty to his liege, the supreme virtue in the code of Bushido. His mother, boasting a distant samurai ancestor, had inculcated that notion to her son, but his father, Eugène had once confided to A.S., was a maker of tofu, of bean-curd, in the outskirts of Kyoto. Be that as it may, Eugène had served his master seven years with only one week's vacation a year, at Christmas. Now, he wanted to return to Japan for a visit. In those days, it would have required a train trip to Marseilles, or perhaps to Genoa, and the best part of two weeks at sea until Yokohama came into sight. If you double this and add a three-week stay in Kyoto, it would be an absence of almost three months.

One can imagine Eugène in his pantry, painstakingly polishing silver and thinking how to approach A.S. with his request; coming to a decision, taking off his apron, and slipping into his striped yellow and black waistcoat, adjusting the knot of his black tie, and taking a deep breath.

We know that A.S. dismissed the request. It wasn't unreasonable, but how could he, Antoine Steinberg, with his precise habits, demands, exigencies, and quirks, manage to live alone for three months? It was impossible to imagine such an eventuality, and it's surprising that it should have been voiced at all. Eugène certainly bowed in acknowledgment, but not very deeply.

Late one afternoon two months later, A.S. returned home from his gallery on the Quai de Conti: he would change before going to his club and thence to a dinner party. His clothes had been impeccably laid out, the right pair of shoes had been selected, all was in order, as usual. A.S. took a shower, changed, and casually said goodnight to Eugène who opened the front door to let him out. "He doesn't look quite right," thought A.S. "I hope he's not coming down with something."

Breakfast was served the following morning, oolong tea, thin toast lightly buttered while it was still warm, and Cooper's marmalade. "What's wrong? Why is he shuffling?" thought A.S.

At day's end, he went directly from the gallery to his club and mentioned his quandary to a fellow member who knew Eugène. "I can't quite make him out," A.S. said. "Nothing wrong with my eyesight, but I seem to see my old servant for the first time. It's ridiculous." By the time he got home it was late and Eugène had gone to bed.

But at breakfast, Antoine Steinberg looked up at his long-time retainer and said: "Are you the Eugène who's been with me the past seven years?"

"No, Monsieur," answered the Japanese, "Eugène is on his way to Japan. He engaged me—you notice that we have the same height, about the same age—he paid my wages for almost two months to come here every day while you were at work, and I know the tiniest details of your likes and dislikes. I will serve you as my friend did, and Eugène will come back to you."

Antoine's reaction was violent.

"This is outrageous. You're an impostor. How dare you and Eugène mount such a farce? You make me look utterly ridiculous. You're dismissed. You leave now!"

Once at his desk at the gallery, A.S. called the personnel agency that had found Eugène for him, and was reputed one of the best in Paris. It was run by a woman and A.S. insisted on speaking to her.

"*Mais oui*, Monsieur Steinberg," she said, "I know everything about this. Your Eugène confided in me and I encouraged him. You are not a good man, Monsieur, and you have lost an admirable servant. Don't ever bother to call me again. I can do nothing for you. Good-day, Monsieur."

17

Bullfight

I once strayed from my calling and engaged in both directing and producing commercials for television—a period that
lasted a couple of years and that a friend labeled my "sordid
past." I also shot several documentaries, but time and effort
were mostly spent on commercials lasting from thirty to sixty
seconds. In truth, I loathed the whole process along with the
people I had to work with. When asked what I did for a living, I'd say that I was "in the movies"; if pressed for details,
that I directed films; and to answer the question "Big budget films?" I'd take the budget of the one-minute commercial
I was directing and multiply it by ninety, an hour-and-a-
half being the average length of a feature. It was an impressive budget.

The strangest commission that ever came my way was
aimed at demonstrating the toughness of a plastic film that
was manufactured in the United States and used to wrap and
protect the carcasses of animals after they had been slaughtered in abattoirs. (The commercial was directed at professionals in the trade.) The New York advertising agency
handling the account called me in Paris and shipped over a
storyboard by Fedex. I agreed to produce and direct the proj-

ect, and they accepted my budget. It turned out to be a substantial production.

The shooting was to take place in Arles, a town in Provence, famous for its Roman amphitheatre now used almost exclusively for bullfights. I rented it for two days. I also purchased two bulls—specially bred in the nearby Camargue region for the *corrida*—along with the services of their *gardians*, as the local cowboys are called; and engaged the services of a *torero* and his three *banderilleros*, his acolytes, for a day. Finally I lined up a film crew and made the necessary arrangements for the shoot's technical needs—cameras, film, lighting. I foresaw using cameras placed at different angles to cover close-ups as well as wider views.

Two rolls of the plastic wrap were shipped by air cargo from the States. The stuff was thick, transparent, and very heavy. The day before the shoot, two tractors had stretched it tight across the arena, effectively cutting the space in two by means of a see-through wall five feet high. Sites for the cameras were chosen.

Three of the manufacturer's representatives arrived from the United States, and from the New York advertising agency, the account executive, the copy writer, the art director, and a stylist. The torero and his three banderilleros, as well as the gardians, were all from Arles, but my crew of eight came down by train from Paris. Hotel and restaurant bookings had been made well in advance.

•

It was mid-afternoon, and the light was perfect—warm, modulated, and casting longish shadows. Everything was in place. I stood in the presiding dignitary's loge, walkie-talkie in hand, the Americans behind me. At last I signaled the three cameras to start rolling and the gardians to release the first bull.

The torero, dressed in his *traje de luces*, his traditional "suit of lights," and his team stood on one side of the plastic; the bull erupted at full speed on the opposite side, slowed down, looked around, and then charged, head down, as soon as it spotted the torero waving his red *capote*. The bull hit the wall. One of its horns pierced the plastic and ripped it. The animal disentangled itself, and resumed the attack. The *cuadrilla*—the torero and his three servers—skillfully induced it toward the opening that led to its pen. The bull must have decided that enough was enough, because it turned around and rushed home. A long pause ensued to allow the tractors to stretch a new transparent wall. The second bull was then released, but this time the wall didn't rip open. It resisted the animal's charge, and the bull, all fourteen hundred pounds, bounced back and ended up sitting on its haunches. The routine, using the two bulls in turn, was kept up for over an hour, the cameras recording alternately success and failure, until I gave the signal for the end of the shoot, "It's a wrap!" The Americans applauded.

A table had been booked at L'Oustau de Baumanière, a three-star restaurant, in the village of Les Baux, twenty minutes away. The landscape, craggy and dramatic, was the perfect setting for this sixteenth-century farmhouse. I'd made reservations for twelve—the client and the agency people, some members of my crew, and the torero. I'd also ordered the menu and chosen the wines. The food was as refined and remarkable as the service was elegant and unobtrusive. The day, in brief, was a success.

I called for the bill, and the headwaiter brought a pewter platter on which rested an ancient leather-bound book. He placed it by my side. The pages of the book had been gouged out to produce a box, inside which I found the bill. It was substantial, but I had foreseen that, and had stealthily buried an estimated amount in my proposal of production expenses. The book-and-platter idea was silly and pretentious, but out of curiosity I tried to pick up the book to read its title on the spine: in vain, because book and platter were bolted together. Tilting my head, I saw it was *The Book of Job*, and the headwaiter said, "Monsieur, that was not my idea."

As I wrote out a check, it occurred to me that I was the owner of two fighting bulls. What could have happened to them? I put the question to the torero. "They went straight to the abattoir," he answered.

I could hardly believe it.

"You must understand, a bullfight is a race against time. It takes a few minutes before the bull gets the idea that it's not the red cloth it should get its horns into, but the torero. Now these two bulls are close to knowing what must really be done, and they'll never forget it. If they got back into the arena, they'd be very dangerous."

The cuadrilla, I supposed, pocketed the proceeds from the sale of my bulls to the butcher, but I wasn't about to make a fuss. Instead, I reflected on the old saying "Knowledge is power." In this case, it had been turned on its head: the poor beasts had been fast learners and paid for it with their lives.

18

The Three Pagoda Pass

"We'd like to help you," said the vestals of the Thai Organization for Tourism, the T.O.T., "but we don't want to lose you. We understand why you want to go there, but the place is riddled with bandits, disease, and wild beasts." Eventually they gave in, but one of their guides would have to come along. No one, that is, no ex-prisoner of war, had ever followed the River Mae Nam Khwae Noi—more generally known as the River Kwai—and what's left of the "Death Railway" to the Three Pagoda Pass, the border between Thailand and Burma. I was contemplating a book based on my diary from 1943, the year I'd spent in the work camps along the river; the notes of this 1979 journey could serve as a counterpoint to my war reminiscences.

Those work camps were strung out a few miles south of the border, and for most of us the Pass and its name evoked the image of an idyllic village surmounted by a craggy rock and white pagodas. I'd seen it twice and it had been a let-down: three dilapidated pagodas that looked as if they'd been made of papier-mâché stood at the edge of the jungle along a flat and dusty road. A tree trunk planed down flat on one side announced in Japanese the name of the Pass. But now, I heard, it was controlled by Mon guerrillas and thrived as the entry point for contraband goods into Burma. The Mons are one of the ethnic groups fighting for their independence from the central government in Rangoon. They'd played a great and glorious role in Burmese history. The Burmese military had been evicted from the border area, the Thais didn't control it, and that surely was the reason for T.O.T.'s reluctance to see me go there.

I was to meet the guide at Kanchanaburi (site of the steel bridge which, for tourism reasons, is presented as the movie bridge, but is not) and rather than ride the train, I took the Class A Luxury bus from Bangkok, a two-hour trip. My choice wasn't only dictated by the heat—April is the worst month of the year—but also by the memory of the "rice trucks," as we called the small steel wagons that were so cramped that we had to take turns sitting during the seven-day journey from Singapore. The bus was air-conditioned, smiling hostesses offered iced drinks and spicy snacks, and above the driver's seat, set in a bower of frangipani, pictures of the King, the Queen, and the Lord Buddha looked down on the passengers.

On arrival, I met the guide at the bus station. He told me to call him Peter, his Thai name being too complicated for a foreigner. Peter had booked two seats in a VW Microbus due to depart that afternoon. We ended up leaving three days later. We made it all the way to Tha-Khanun, seventy-five miles from Kanchanaburi, and halfway to the Burmese border—an excruciating thirteen hours, the wheels plowing into a ribbon of fine white dust. The windows were kept tightly shut and caulked with old rags, it was hot enough inside the bus to bake a loaf of bread, and at journey's end we did look like the baguettes of Provence covered in white flour. The morning after our arrival, Peter came to tell me that the District Officer wanted to see us. The D.O. was all smiles. He offered us tea and cakes. He wanted to help. Unfortunately, no one had managed to reach the Three Pagoda Pass in years. Beyond Tha-Khanun, the road petered to a mere track, and if we found a jeep it would cost us two thousand U.S. dollars just to overhaul it at the end of the trip. Did Peter, instructed by T.O.T., denounce me, or did the D.O. receive a radio message with orders to stop me from going further? Whichever, three days later, I was back in Bangkok.

The luxury bus had been a mistake. If my aim was to summon the remembrance of things past, then my travels needed to be in harmony with their avowed aim. Invoking the spirits (and in this case they were fearful ones) required a ritual I'd ignored.

The new plan called, at first, for two train rides: Bangkok-Kanchanaburi followed by Kanchanaburi-Nam Tok on the narrow-gauge line left over from the "Death Railway"—75 miles out of a total of 350 built in eighteen months at the cost of 150,000 lives. The travel arrangements had been conveyed to me by the Jacques Bes representative in Bangkok. Bes was a Frenchman who ran a raft-hotel on the river, at a place called Kinsayok. I would be met at Nam Tok and taken by boat to the rafts. Thence, accompanied by a Mon, I'd make my way by any means available to the Three Pagoda Pass. As soon as I entered Mon controlled territory, the Mon guerrillas would take care of me.

•

Jacques is waiting for me at Nam Tok, as arranged. We have a beer and board his boat. From the six-cylinder Chrysler engine amidships, a ten-foot propeller shaft extends to the rear, allowing the slim craft to navigate the shallows. When the sun hits the spume arcing off the stern, the boat trails a splendid rainbow, an oversized and wildly iridescent dragonfly. Getting to Kinsayok takes almost two hours, winding through a corridor of thick vegetation. The first of many white cones, the geologist's "inselberg," rises around a bend, and the river looks like a Chinese print. A buffalo scampers up the banks. A grey punt, from which a man and a woman are fishing, rocks in our wake. Waterfalls crash into the river, and swifts streak out of limestone caves. Past and present now connect. Images coalesce, those of 1943 and of 1979.

When I was a prisoner, reads the journal I wrote in Kwai camps, "looking down on that river at dawn, fog skimming the water, mist ascending in soft billows over the jungle; listening to the cries of invisible birds, and sometimes hearing the distant trumpeting of an elephant, helped one to remember the first commandment, *Primum Vivere*. The experience, just like the sun that was soon to dispel fog and mist, cleared doubts at those moments when hopelessness pushed you down the dark and slippery tunnel. The reaffirmation came seldom. But when it did, it brought a great silence." I equated this silence with happiness, and at the time I could have been absolutely right.*

For the last stage of the journey, Aung Song, my young Mon companion, gets us a ride on the back of a truck carrying both goods and locals. We've been traveling for a couple of weeks, walking, cadging rides on trucks or even on bullock-carts. Occasionally, Aung Song reveals my connection with the region, causing a group to form around me, groping, touching, pinching, making sure I'm not a ghost, expressing amazement that I've survived. A man in the truck says, "Every day boom-boom at two o'clock: America and English planes." A girl comes and sits close to me. Behind a Princeton University tee shirt she has the most beautiful breasts, bouncing like everything and everyone in the truck. "Watch out," says Aung Song, "she's the driver's wife."

* From *To the River Kwai, Two Journeys, 1943, 1979*, op. cit.

We cross the border. The three pagodas have been white-washed, and a wire has been stretched across their elegant spires; attached to the wire, burned-out electric bulbs add a contemporary touch. The Phra Chedi, the three pagodas, were erected in the eighteenth century by the kings of Siam and Burma who signed a covenant of eternal peace at the foot of the central one. Monks in yellow robes wave at us from the entrance of a small monastery in the rear of the pagodas. A larger one is being built near by.

A mile down from the Pass, we stop at the village—the village that the prisoners imagined in their romantic fantasies. From the 1979 diary:

> The thatched houses with their verandahs and flower-ing bushes nestle in bowers of lacy bamboo groves; the fronds of large trees arch over the roofs; and through the smoke of charcoal fires the sun's slanting rays throw splotches of blue light . . . Outside the three general stores, which double up as inns, people meet to shop and gossip and bare-bottom children play soldiers on

the doorsteps of houses. A bullock-cart delivers a sack of rice to be husked and polished at the door of the mill, humming and murmuring all day long. Coveys of small pink pigs root in the ditches, and hump-backed oxen drift about, lazily nibbling away at clumps of grass. Sitting in deep puddles, water-buffalos ruminate.*

Our arrival is expected, for as we get off the truck a boy in Mon uniform tells us to report to the depot of the MNLA— the Mon National Liberation Army. The MNLA rules life in this village. It also controls the contraband trade: bullock-cart convoys carrying contraband goods follow the jungle track into Burma. They return with cattle, rubies, gold, silver, and jade. During the monsoon season, elephants replace the bullock carts.

The depot is a two-story teak house. We're greeted by the vice chairman of the Mon State Party, a captain, and two lieutenants, and told to store our bedding under the altar to the Buddha, next to an array of light weapons stacked along the walls. Tea is poured from a Chinese thermos decorated with chubby little girls, and Aung Song accepts an offer of betel nut that a man is slicing with a giant cigar-cutter. The captain asks how long I plan to stay here. My aim, I tell him, is to see the steel bridge that I was told was still standing at Apalon, forty kilometers beyond the border Jacques had mentioned to me, explaining that the decision would be the guerrillas' and would depend on the presence—or rather the absence—of Burmese Army patrols in the vicinity. The vice chairman, who's been silent so far, suddenly speaks up, "Permission is granted. You leave tomorrow with this captain and an escort." Food is brought on: a curry of wild deer, roast boar, fish, and vegetables. The village headman arrives to tell

* From *To the River Kwai, Two Journeys, 1943, 1979*, op. cit.

us that dances are planned in my honor tonight . . . "You are an original inhabitant of Phra Chedi," he says.

Night is falling. "I move from house to house and watch the actors making up by the light of candles and oil lamps. In their dark huts, these men and women I've seen in the fields barefoot and in tatters, sit on a mat, small mirrors propped up against the bamboo wall, and transmute themselves into ancient courtiers. Gold and silver dust, white pomades, lipsticks, black eye makeup, rouge, unguents of green, mauve, and yellow hues and colored talcums are taken out of their tiny wood and metal boxes. Slowly, almost languorously, they are applied with finger and paintbrush on forehead, eyebrows, eyelids, cheeks, and mouths."* From boxes and battered suitcases, sumptuous clothes are extracted. I take photographs and marvel at the slow transformation of these Asian peasants into gods, high priests, and delicious princesses.

A stage has been constructed off the road, with a space cleared to accommodate the spectators. Acetylene lamps

---

* From *To the River Kwai, Two Journeys, 1943, 1979,* op. cit.

throw a cold, hard light, deepening the darkness of the jungle all around. The show will start at nine P.M., and by the time I arrive, half an hour before "the curtain goes up," the food and betel nut vendors are already doing business. Everyone is seated on the ground, the Mon garrison standing at the back in case of a Burmese attack.

Below the stage, fifteen musicians wait in the orchestra pit. The drummer is the leader, a large wooden barrel and eighteen small drums lined up in front of him. He announces the opening with a roll of thunder to which answer cymbals, and reeds of different pitches, an echo of Balinese gamelan instructed in the distant past by Chinese court music. One by one, the dancers present themselves, advancing in mincing steps to the front of the platform where they freeze in convoluted poses.

The first round announces in song and dance that we're to be transported to the court of the Mon King in his capital, Pegu. This is the eighteenth century. Applause and shouts of admiration greet the appearance of green- and plum-colored silks, peacock blue calicoes, feathered headdresses, the glitter and the pearls. Drawing from each one his own excellence, the head dancer leads a turn with each of the forty performers.

Now unfold the stories of war-obsessed kings, of immensely wise monkey-priests, and compassionate elephants. The lithe bodies of men and women move sinuously against a naïve backdrop of palaces and pagodas. Undulating hands, polychrome faces, bird-like heads crowned in feathers, provocative eyes—Asiatic sensualities and archaic memories embodied in these Mon peasants who, wanting to honor me, have recalled in a jungle clearing the past glories of their King and his people.

Humbly, I thank the performers, the villagers, and the village chief. The dances have lasted three and a half hours.

19

Black Beauty

Deià's beach calls for agility and the acceptance of a little pain: After negotiating a couple of wooden ladders set against a steep cliff you'll find yourself hopping on largish stones, though rounded and smoothed out by eons on the sea bed. No fine, white sand, which probably saves the place from mass tourism. However, Deià, on the coast of Majorca, is famous as Robert Graves's home for many years until his death in 1985, and for the so-called creative people, mostly foreigners, who have chosen to live there.

I first saw this ancient fishing village sitting on a hill in the early 1980s. We were staying, the then woman of my heart and I, in a *finca*, an old farmhouse owned by a writer friend of hers. The beach, he'd warned us, was strictly nudist, and my companion said, "Go if you want to, but without me."

So I got hold of a book and a towel, followed the path on top of the cliff, and was about to go down the ladders when I noticed two girls already engaged on the lower rungs. Naked, uniformly tanned by the sun, both sporting (as the strange expression goes) neat, black, and well trimmed pubic triangles. I watched them climb up, pleasurably trying to imagine what the late General Francisco Franco would have thought of it.

Once on the beach, I stripped, laid myself down on the towel, opened my book, and discreetly looked over clusters of young people, most of them as attractive as the ladder's slim beauties—a reminder of Leni Riefenstahl, Hitler's favorite filmmaker, and her early documentaries of "Strength through Joy" athletes, deeply tanned, long-limbed, and naked.

A very young woman walked by me on her way to the sea. She was black, naked, but her blackness was of a deep, elephant grey. Strikingly, it was an overall color, whether on face, buttocks, or hair—and matte, without a hint of sheen. She took supple strides on her finely muscled African legs, seemingly weightless, as if by some strange alchemy she was defeating gravity. Her back was perpendicular to the ground and in line with an elongated neck. The face itself had none of the Negroid features associated with Central Africa. She was, I believed, either a Rwandan Tutsi or perhaps a Somali, though I settled her for a Nuba, the most beautiful people on earth who live in the Sudan. I fancied her as the descendant of women who, bearing amphorae of oil, once walked along the green banks of the Nile, who strode on the sands of the Red Sea, tall baskets of mangoes and guavas in perfect balance on their oval heads. She was the pubescent girl bedded by King Solomon, the Sultan's favorite in the Topkapi harem, the Queen of Sheba, the irresistible slave girl of Orientalist painters.

My black goddess entered the sea and swam away with powerful breaststrokes. Lifting my eyes from the book, I constantly glanced toward the sea to watch the shadowy silhouette of her head bobbing in and out of the sparkling waves. At last she turned to the shore, reached the shallows, and stood up. I had mistaken another swimmer for her: I was looking at a white girl. But no, she was the black goddess, now transmogrified into a healthy, suntanned, blond-haired girl, stepping carefully on the beach stones as she walked past me to rejoin her friends.

I soon noticed people making their way toward a spot close to the ladders at the back of the beach. There, from a cleft in the cliff's wall, deep grey mud oozed out into a small pool, a deep grey mud that people smeared all over their bodies, and that dried with the even matte color I'd so much admired.

Of all our sexual organs, the brain, it's been said, is the most active, inventive, and prolific. Mine—both the reptilian and the median—had presented me wondrous images of the Ur girl. She had shed them all in the waters of the warm blue sea.

20

Veronicas

Legend has it that a woman named Veronica gave her veil to Christ on his way to Golgotha. When Christ handed it back after wiping his perspiring face, his image was imprinted on the veil. In the seventeenth century, Francisco de Zurbarán produced seven versions—large oil paintings—of various foldings of cloth bearing the Face. One of these foldings was used as a model by Jean-Baptiste Oudry, Louis XV's *animalier* painter (animals were his favorite subject): it became the background against which hangs a hare that has been snared or shot. Then again, the Philadelphia artist Raphaelle Peale produced a painting in 1822, *Venus Rising from the Sea—A Deception*, in which the Zurbarán folds hide the figure of a nude woman of whom we see only face and shoulders as well as a hint of legs. In 1975, I spent a whole day in the studio over the ironing board in an attempt to reproduce that particular Zurbarán rendition of a linen cloth. It took but a few minutes to photograph "The Great Cloth," leaving out the figure of Christ, the hare, and Venus. Inevitably, Veronica became the patron saint of photographers—*vera icon*, the true image—while in the bullring, *veronica* describes a movement of the cape as the bull charges past the torero.

Over the following two decades, once a year I attempted to produce a new version of The Great Cloth, but none measured up to it, until it all became a frustrating ritual. I had long noticed the fixation of both sculptors and painters for folded fabric, whether in draperies or clothing. In Pharaonic sculptures, in the apsaras of Angkor Wat, or in the extravagance of Baroque paintings, the infinite intricacies of fabric and draperies were clearly an obsession—Leonardo's celebrated series of draped figures being surely the most astonishing for both sharpness of vision and execution. Was the rendition of folded fabric a demonstration of the artist's skill, or was it the closest to abstract art that the times allowed?

When I came across chaos theory, I saw how it fitted with the infinite variants of folded cloth. This resulted in two years of putting together a body of work that reflected the theory, and ending up as a large coffee-table book.* After the interminable gestation that followed my first "Veronica," suddenly and without much effort, I produced another ten versions, using new and different configurations as well as a variety of fabrics. I traveled to India (turbans, saris, Kathakali dancers); to Tibet (monks and prayer flags); to Berlin when Christo wrapped the Reichstag; crossed the Atlantic on a ninety-foot ketch (sails); worked in the studio, in my house in Provence, and of course in Paris where I lived.

---

* Chaos theory deals mathematically with random and exceedingly complicated configurations, such as a gushing stream, clouds, or a rugged coastline. Minute disturbances can change the aspect of these configurations—hence the often quoted "butterfly effect," whereby theoretically a butterfly flying off a bush in Beijing might change the weather pattern in New York. A slight turn of your wrist will alter the folds of your shirt, but never, even in the infinity of time, will they return to their exact previous state. Yet they will forever appear to be the folds of a cotton shirt, never to be mistaken for anything else, such as a stream of lava or molten metal.

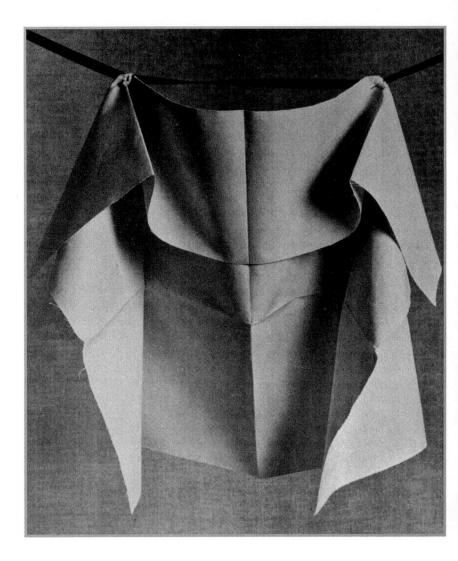

I discovered and illustrated (nudes and bed sheets) the
work of the French psychoanalyst Gaëtan Gatian de Clérambault whose book, *Erotic Passion for Cloth in Women,* had
brought him notoriety in Paris before the First World War.
Whenever a woman was arrested for stealing a length of silk
from a store, Clérambault was called in. These women, he

found out, pleasured themselves through the feel of silk, although for the sought effect it had to be stolen, or else nothing happened.

Clérambault, a medical officer in the French armed forces, was twice wounded in the early stages of the First World War. Invalided out of the army, he was posted to Morocco where he took thousands of photographs of Arab women in their burkas, only the eyes and occasionally hennaed hands remaining visible. He never showed these pictures to anyone. For him they were pornographic: he saw clothing as a sexual skin that could be put on or taken off at will.

I gathered texts and quotes to accompany the photographs, writings as diverse as their authors—Aldous Huxley, Leibnitz, Mallarmé, Deleuze, and others. The thesaurus provided over 250 appellations for cloth—grogram, shalloon, tussah, mackinaw—and a plethora of verbs to describe its shapes— swagged, crêped, billowed, wimpled.

Most mysterious was the quote from Ecclesiastes 4:5, to accompany a photograph of a napkin folded into a fool's hat: "The fool foldeth his hands together, and eateth his own flesh." And the legend I most cherished was Japanese. Amaterasu, the Sun Goddess, struck the ocean waters with her wand. As she raised her hand, drops fell back into the sea to become the islands of Japan. The Goddess knew that men would eventually appear on these islands, and she went to her spinning wheel. She spun cloth, for man is the only creature on this planet that crucially and irremediably needs cloth.

21

Stalking and Smoking

To find the landing strip using only visual navigation was a feat. Deserts offer few points of reference, and now for more than two hours we'd been hovering—or so it felt—over the Kalahari, peering down at an unending carpet of bushes studded with an occasional acacia tree. The vegetation soaked in the light of the sun, and disorientation became twinned with anxiety. Not the anxiety that comes from flying in rough weather, or the knowledge that small planes are more prone to fatal accidents, or the possibility of a crash landing in the terrain below. It was angst, floating anxiety, as shapeless as the land, as diffused as the light. When the Cessna started to descend and the landing gear rumbled into place and a cluster of tents came into view, the eye found a point of reference and the anxiety instantly vanished.

We taxied up the landing strip to a battered Army truck. A tall man with a sun-scorched face and a shock of grey-blond hair struggling under an Aussie hat stood by the cab. "Yes, I'm Jim," was all he said by the way of introduction. We'd heard about him: ex-Colonial Office who in the past had served in Botswana and now took people on safaris in the Kalahari Desert. ("Safari parks, safari holidays, safari adventures." I hated these tourist-brochure words.) The Bushmen were his friends.

The day after our arrival, everyone slept late. The pilot had flown off at dawn, and of our group of six only Jacqueline and I showed up at breakfast. Jim suggested we go stalking for kudu. Jacqueline, who was imbued with the mystique of the hunt, would have opted for shooting, but I'd always been intrigued by the idea of stalking, where, in order to come close to the "prey" (as close as possible, but not in order to kill it), you have to observe its behavior, appreciate its mode of apprehension. In brief, you have to identify with the animal itself. Stalking requires self-control and concentrates the mind in a pool of great quiet. My own experience of stalking, however, had been not so much concerned with sport as with survival when, in the jungle during the war, armed with a stick or a stone, I attempted to approach any edible prey—bird, snake, or rat—and kill it. A distant experience from stalking a stag on a Scottish moor.

Jacqueline agreed to Jim's proposition. We also both agreed not to wake the rest of the group and invite them to join us. Anyway, stalking is not a team sport.

Jim and a Bushman sat up front in the cab, Jim at the wheel, Jacqueline and I rattling in the back, and looking out of the canopy. Our Bushman, who'd been given the name of Bob, was a man in his forties, we surmised, no more than five feet tall, a big bushy head of hair, lively eyes, and flattened features. He was dressed in old tattered khaki shorts and a faded red shirt, flip-flops on his feet. A long time ago I'd read Laurens van der Post's *The Lost World of the Kalahari*, and I was curious to check out two of the author's observations, although I didn't remember much else of the book itself. One concerned the genitalia of the male Bushman, always in a state of erection; the other, the genitalia of the female, or

rather a fold of skin that hides her pubis, an anatomical feature known morphologically as *le tablier égyptien*, the Egyptian apron. Evolution, to my mind, had once more admirably
arranged matters: given the permanent priapic state of males,
had the mound of Venus not been hidden, either generalized
rape would have become a way of life, or else the organ would
have ceased to be erotically desirable and this would have
resulted in the obliteration of that variant of our species. I
failed to observe the Bushmen's anatomical wonders, yet I've
seen references to them in the work of a French anthropol-
ogist. For all I know, it may exist in a Bushman tribe other
than Bob's. Or else, like so many widely held beliefs, it's become a "fact" through one account or thesis repeatedly pick-
ing up on another.

After forty-five minutes of roaming through the bush,
mostly following tracks, we came to a sudden stop. Jim and
Bob climbed down, and Bob pointed to a spoor in the dust—
a lion, announced Jim. No, a lioness, corrected Bob. She's not
far away, he said, maybe she's even looking at us. We decided
to forget the kudu, and stalk her instead.

Jim's only weapon was an odd looking rifle, the kind of
thing you'd find in the collection of disparate tools and weapons at the Pitt Rivers Museum in Oxford—not unlike a toy
machine-pistol. It could be dismantled and the barrel inserted
into the stock, and was then small enough to be slipped into
a suitcase. Winston Churchill carried this type of weapon
when he was a journalist in the Boer War. Its small bore, however, would have made it totally inadequate to stop a charging
lioness. Jim would drive back to the camp to get an appropri-
ate weapon, and we'd wait for him in the shade of an acacia,
the Bushman in attendance. An hour later, he returned with
a large bore rifle and a grin on his face. "I could've scalped
them all," he said, "everyone was fast asleep."

We climbed back into the truck. By now the lioness must have outdistanced us and we had to catch up with her. Soon we came across an unmistakable sign of her passage. A dead kudu, belly split open, was spread out on the ground by the side of the track. Bob explained that the animal had not been killed for its meat, but for the water in its stomach. Jacqueline knelt by the carcass, shoed away the flies, brought her nose down, and smelled it with the same expression I'd once seen on the faces of perfume specialists in Grasse. She pulled out her hunting knife and was about to cut off a haunch. I asked her what she thought she was doing.

She looked at me, a glazed expression in her eyes. The hunting mystique had got into her.

"Eat it, of course."

"We'll be on foot from now on," said Jim. "There's no way we're going to carry fifty pounds of meat in this heat. And it's not going into the truck either."

We locked the truck's doors and marched off. The air radiated heat, the light shimmered, the sky glared. There was no landscape, just an unending maze of spiny bushes, shapeless and colorless. We hung handkerchiefs at the back of our hats to protect our necks. Bob was in the lead. He knew precisely where he was; he knew each bush. It was his territory. But if you took him out of it, Jim explained, he would have been as helpless as we were, and if anything happened to him we would die. We would never find the way back to the truck.

We went from acacia to acacia, and saw—or rather we were shown—the marks left by the lioness. She too suffered from the heat and lay down in the shade. When she felt the sun on her, rather than shift and find another shady part of tree, she'd go off and look for a new acacia. Occasionally, Bob would say in an off-handed way, "I know she's looking at us. She's quite close." He read her path, the trace of her pads in the dust. Twisting and turning, he followed her meanderings. He was bent in two, his head down, his index finger pointed at the spoor, as if the finger had a will of its own and was pulling him along.

The day wore on. We could not risk being caught by darkness. By day, except for snakes, there's little danger walking about in the bush: animals shy away from humans (except for the rogue buffalo, the most dangerous African game; there's no way of knowing whether he'll charge or slump away). Nighttime, however, is hunting time for all creatures, and we turn into prey. It's then best to move away from trails and climb up a tree.

Jim was worried. It would take us three hours to return to the truck, and it was time to turn around. We had no food and little water. We reached a depression in the land, almost a gully, with dry, yellowish grass growing above the waist. This would be our ultimate point, we would halt for a rest and then start back. We sat or knelt, heads just above the grass. Bob didn't have to tell us. We knew. The lioness was in front of us. Invisible. Waiting. But no more waiting to pounce on us than we, on our side, intended to shoot her. I felt tension within me, but the tension of perfect equilibrium, an awareness of everything being wonderfully in place, where it should be. The closest thing, I thought, to what a yogi would experience. The silence was simultaneously absolute and alive—not the silence of dusk when the life that thrives in sunlight prepares for sleep, nor the eerie silence of pre-dawn when another life is about to awaken, but the hum of the world.

We suddenly heard the grass rustling, a whoosh in the air, and a dik-dik, the tiny and exquisitely formed bonsai antelope, flew over us in a perfect arc, legs and neck extended, head pointed. The world is forever in motion, and the immobility of perfect balance could not be sustained any longer.

The dik-dik was the instrument of change, and we knew the end was about to be revealed.

The lioness raised her head above the grasses and looked at us. We looked at her. She was no more than twenty feet away. The yellow eyes never blinked—nor ours, I would imagine. This lasted three or four seconds, until slowly, very slowly, her head rose high and she turned around. Her tail flew up, she took a great leap, and disappeared.

•

The following day, we all piled into the truck, the whole group this time, and at Bob's invitation, we drove to his village. From afar we saw a few huts scattered in a rough circle and tall, crooked poles stuck in the ground in haphazard fashion. The wind brought the stench of meat stuck on the poles and drying in the sun. We stopped the truck at the village's entrance. The red earth was strewn with thousands of rusty cans.

Bob's family came to greet us. We were surrounded by open, smiling faces. Everyone was in rags, barefoot, with large splayed feet, broken toenails, and scarred shins. Bob called his brother: they wanted us to see them light a fire by rubbing two pieces of wood together. The brother brought a short stick. Its bark had been peeled off and a shallow hole had been gouged out to receive a pencil-like piece of wood, of another and harder nature than the stick. Bob took off his shirt, squatted, and started to twirl the pencil between the palms of his hands. The effort and the concentration caused rivulets of sweat to roll down his back. A few minutes later, his brother spelled him. Soon a whiff of burning floated in the air, no more than a few carbonized cells, I imagined, so faint was the scent. Bob presented a small dry leaf and a few strands of dried grass where the pencil's point was embedded in the stick. A thread of smoke rose in the still air. The smell of burning became more pronounced, and at last, at last, a minute flame flared up and raced through the dried grass. The brother fell backward, exhausted by the effort. We applauded. We had been silent, watchful, taken back to the quest for fire; humanity was going to survive, our families would be warm in the winter cave, and we would roast our meat.

We offered cigarettes. The Bushmen love smoking. They inhale deeply, desperately, as if it is the last breath of air in the world. Smoke seems to seep out of their ears, their nostrils, and their eyes. It swirls around their head. Bob and his brother each took a cigarette, but we urged them to take at least two for a serious smoke. They thanked us and followed the suggestion. The brother dug his hand in the one serviceable pocket of his shorts and pulled out a Bic disposable lighter. He flicked it and lit up. We laughed and once again clapped our hands: thirty thousand years had elapsed, and man was still around and smoking.

Jim, however, turned on the two Bushmen.

"For Christ's sake," he almost screamed at them, "I've already told you never to do this in front of tourists!"

In disgust, he walked away, back to the truck.

Bob, with a movement of his head, indicated he wanted me to follow him. I entered his hut. He motioned me to squat down, and from under a piece of sack cloth he pulled out an ostrich egg that bore two pictures, a mythical bird and a man riding a wild pig—an egg with magical properties, unlike the ostrich eggs used to store the water sucked through a straw from beneath the parched, sere surface of the desert. He handed it over to me and said, "More for you." The other present was a small, articulated wooden puppet hanging on a string. The string was tied to a thin branch, nicely polished. He demonstrated how to use the toy, holding the branch in the right hand and with the left hitting it with

another, shorter piece of wood. The elasticity of the device caused the puppet to jump, to throw arms and legs in the air, to dance. Why did he choose me for these inestimable gifts? I still don't know.

（22）

Moute-Moute

'm happier in the company of women. They're superior to men, and we've waited too long for them to assert themselves and do the right thing about a world that's going to the dogs. Why do I say that? Because this story is about Cameroon, and if that country is going to get anywhere, it's the women who will take it there—wherever "there" is located.

According to a United Nations survey, Cameroon is right at the top among the winners in the corruption stakes. We got our first lesson immediately after landing at Yaoundé, the capital: the official from the Ministry of Health who came to pick us up at the airport ordered the driver stop at the first filling station, had us pay for the gas, instructed the station attendant to double the actual amount, and finally pocketed the bill for an eventual refund from his ministry. He was also our introduction to *palabre*, or disputative logorrhea. Multi-syllable words illustrate verbal curlicues, proverbs accompany fables, and euphemisms mingle with illustrative anecdotes. The effect is that of a vast and senseless baroque construction. It can be entertaining at first, but it soon pales.

I was in Cameroon with Frédéric, my Paris cameraman, to shoot three documentaries for the Helen Keller Foundation, an American NGO whose aim is to eradicate river blindness or onchocerciasis. All over East and Central Africa, a little black fly known locally as the *moute-moute* breeds along lakes and rivers. It deposits its eggs under the skin of humans, and in time the larvae make their way to the eyes, destroying the optic nerve and causing blindness. They can also produce such a painful body itch that people have been known to commit suicide. Fearing the effects of the fly, farmers abandon the cultivation of land close to rivers, which is often the most productive.

In 1996, the pharmaceutical firm Merck Sharp & Dohme brought out Mectizan, a remedy against river blindness. One pill gives protection for a year. The company provides it free of charge to the countries that require it, in any quantity and as long as they need it. In Cameroon, Helen Keller is responsible for its distribution at a cost of around ten dollars per pill. The figure appears extravagant, but the NGO has to set up an infrastructure to train nurses, send volunteer workers who spread information about the disease, visit distant regions, and finally dispense the pills. The documentaries I'd been commissioned to produce were to be used for the training of volunteer workers, for the education of villagers, and for fund-raising.

The NGO had detailed Jérémie to stay at our side. Without him, we would have been unable to function. He was our factotum, guide, and trouble-shooter, and yet he was a simple soul, open-minded to the point of naivety. If ever his mistress, he assured us, told him she'd found someone willing to marry her, he wouldn't try to talk her out of it; he'd let her go. He didn't want to spoil the chances for happiness of a woman who under different circumstances might have been his wife. In brief, he wasn't the marrying type. These simple thoughts were voiced as if they'd been Schopenhauer's moral injunctions.

In the course of an introductory tour, Jérémie took us to visit a village deep in the forest. It was noon, and no one was about—not a grandmother taking care of a baby, not an old man sitting in front of his hut. Everyone was out working in the cocoa plantations. Jérémie had heard of a local dispensary in the vicinity, but we could find no sign of it. Driving once more across the wide, empty space in the center of the village, we saw a man with a cane looking around him with a proprietary air as if the village was part of his estate. A large and imposing man, he wore a three-piece suit the color of a ripe banana. Equally striking were a bright fuchsia shirt and a violently colored striped tie. On his feet he had white-and-tan shoes, and on his head, the stiff straw hat known as a boater. We stopped the Land Rover and asked him where we could find the dispensary. Grandly—our rough clothing betrayed our lowly status—he announced, *"Moi, Mossieur, je souis de Pawis. Je souis un touwiste."* A Parisian tourist. No help whatsoever.

Jérémie was our guide, but our driver was Pascal, skilled, silent, and unruffled. It was only when the big lumber trucks came roaring down the jungle track, and he'd swerve our car off the track and into the forest, that he let fly in Cameroon patois, or else in French for our benefit. Pascal was light-skinned, and lithe to the point of flimsiness. He was also quick-witted. He had become enamored of Bébé Madeleine, a beautiful woman who had written a play performed in villages to teach people how to combat river blindness and to trust the yearly white pill rather than the local witch doctor or the sorceress around the corner. I in turn had asked her to adapt her play for a cinematic treatment. Bébé Madeleine was massive. Yet she moved graciously, and her maroon skin had a delicious satiny gloss. At last, she decided to rid Pascal of all hope.

"Your looks!" she said, "they're written all over your face—you'd like to fuck me. Don't think of it, Pascal. With my weight I'd squash you flat."

Pascal closed his right fist, lifting the tip of his little finger. "A tiny bullet can kill an elephant," he said, closing his left eye as if he was about to take aim.

Jérémie wanted us to meet his family and have dinner with his father and mother. For the sake of good relations we accepted, and one day after work we drove to Jérémie's village.

It was early evening, and the heat of the day had hardly abated. The village presented the usual helter-skelter of sheds and houses with corrugated tin roofs, compounds for cattle, and a church. The church doors were in the shape of a traditional gothic arch and were daubed with the word SHALOM written large in white paint.

Pascal stopped the car at the entrance of a goat pen. An old man in jeans and a faded red shirt raced out of the house. It was Jérémie's father. He embraced us, and led us inside the goat pen. It was in fact the patio of his house, and occasionally the local discothèque. Several people seated at a table stood up when we entered. They were all men, except for one woman, our guide's mother, dressed in a black muumuu splashed with a pattern of vivid flowers. We were given glasses of palm wine and introduced to the schoolteacher, the priest, Jérémie's older brother, and an uncle. Everyone, with the exception of the mother, was clearly under the influence, and throughout the evening, the cultivation of the palm, its care, its harvest, the fermentation of the wine, and its con-

Shalom Church

sumption were the exclusive subject of conversation. When the occasion presented itself, I asked the priest the significance of the word painted on the church doors. His voice sounded as if it reverberated inside a cave.

"That," he said, "is an Arab word. It means 'God is Great.' I painted it on the door myself because the Israelis are bad people."

"Bad people," repeated the father. "Let's drink a toast to the Arabs. Shalom!"

We all said "Shalom!" and drank.

A large couscous was brought to the table. Bones and parts of unidentifiable animals floated in the gravy. It was highly spiced and had lost all affinity with its Moroccan origin. Its local name is *fourretout*, "stuff everything." The couscous label was no doubt meant to spare our Western sensibilities. The mother doled out generous portions, and we praised its excellence.

"She made it," exclaimed the father. "She's my number one wife, my best, and the mother of my children. The mother of Jérémie. Let's drink to her."

We drank.

"Of course, I've got other wives. Younger, and more children by them."

Number One wife looked down at her plate.

We drank a toast to wives.

The evening wore on, we kept drinking, candles were lit, the laughter got louder, and the talk about the making of palm wine more passionate. Jérémie attempted to divert the conversation to river blindness and Mectizan.

"*Pas toucher!*" said the schoolteacher, don't get anywhere near it.

When I asked why, he replied that the side effects were bad. "How bad?"

"*La mort*," death.

By the time we left, with the promise of a prompt return, Frédéric and I had splitting headaches. Pascal drove us back without a word. He'd hardly said anything all evening. He made it no secret; he held these people in contempt.

From early morning until nightfall, with a midday break, we interviewed village chiefs, filmed volunteer workers, and recorded the distribution of the pills. One day, having finished work early, we dismissed both Pascal and Jérémie and returned to the little town where we'd established our base, some 150 kilometers from Yaounde. Rather than retire to our dingy hotel rooms, we went to the marketplace, to a bar with a large verandah. We'd have a beer and read until dinnertime. We chose a table at one end of the verandah where we could catch a faint breeze. There was no one in the place, except for three girls in the far corner. The most striking of the three wore a satin dress of glaring green with a large hat of the same color. An imposing and shapely bosom pouted below her neckline. A slim girl in a skimpy black sheath was the youngest. The third wore a simple white dress. All three looked smart and had straightened hair.

Frédéric had his back turned to the girls, whereas I was facing them. Skimpy-sheath was sending signals, unmistakably asking to be invited to our table. I didn't respond, and she came over on her own. We asked her to sit down, and she ordered a beer. Her name was Solo Star, she said, exhibiting on the inside of her arm the tattoo of a star and the two words of her adopted name. Solo Star was as pretty as she was lively. Her French was perfect and her English passable. She had bold eyes, and the skin of her thighs, which she crossed and uncrossed in a provocative way, looked like fine black silk. She cuddled up to me, and in no time at all she suggested that she'd make me an excellent wife. She'd have no problem adapting to life in Paris.

It wasn't very nice of us, she implied, to leave her two friends alone, and before we could say a thing, she'd beckoned them over to our table. The green dress was named Félicité and the white one, Patricia. They were half sisters, whereas Félicité and Solo Star had the same mother and father. Complications and permutations are so prevalent in Cameroon that relationships must be qualified: Félicité and Solo Star were sisters *père-mère*.

Drinks were ordered and the banter resumed. Of course, said the girls, we're going to have dinner together, and then "we'll come and have a look at your rooms." Tomorrow night, we suggested, would be more suitable, as tonight we were to have an "important dinner with government people," and we couldn't very well bring the girls along. They might have been professionals, but more likely they were just out to boost their income. However enticing we found them, the notion of AIDS somehow chilled our libido.

"Anyway, I'm sure you've never had real Cameroon food," said Solo Star.

"That's where you're wrong," I said. "Three nights ago we did." She asked how and where, and I related the dinner with Jérémie's family.

"You're quite sure?" asked Solo Star, looking at the others with a grin, "Was it in the village with SHALOM on the church door?"

"It was," I replied. "A landmark."

Howls of laughter. "But we know who you are! You're the two whites working with our brother Jérémie!"

We couldn't believe it.

"What's the population of Cameroon?" asked Frédéric.

"Thirteen million," said Félicité.

"It's a small world!"

A new round of beers was ordered. I asked the girls to tell us what they did and what they wanted out of life.

"You've seen what it's like at home," said Patricia, who'd kept mostly in the background. "Well, we don't want to be like our mother. She works in the fields, she works in the house, she looks after the kids, she cooks, and I wouldn't be surprised if papa had asked her to help his younger wives. And you saw how she's treated? *C'est pas possible!*"

"That's just what we don't want," said Félicité.

"*Moi, je dis merde à tout ça,*" said Solo Star. Fuck all that.

Félicité's hope was to work as a hotel clerk; Patricia was interested in nursing; Solo Star thought that running a dress shop would suit her. "That's if you don't take me back to Paris," she added.

All of this required money for training. There was only one quick way of obtaining it.

I congratulated them and said that if there was some hope for the country to straighten itself out it would surely come from the efforts of women. We admired these three girls, Frédéric and I, and we made an appointment with them for dinner the next day at the best restaurant in town. We wanted to help them, and they promised we'd have fun. The next day, it started to rain heavily, the electricity was cut off all over town in late afternoon, and the two whites had a cold dinner on their own by the light of a candle.

23

The Dollar

Fortune magazine in New York signed me up shortly after I'd pinned on myself the label of photographer. When I look back on it, technically I was a primitive, but as long as I could work with a Leica and natural light, I felt unafraid.

Fear, it turned out, was a problem for some of the photographers sent out by the magazine to meet tycoons, captains of industries, and powerful political or financial figures. With the exception of entertainment people, models, and ego-trippers complacent about their looks, no one sits in front of a camera with much pleasure. Unlike movies, where the reverse is necessary, a photograph—a portrait, in particular—has to be slightly "over the top." A dramatic or unexpected element must be introduced. This requires some of the skills of a screen or stage director, a measure of control over the sitter. If the person in front of the camera feels a hesitancy or timidity on the part of the photographer, nothing much will happen. The people at *Fortune* had read my cv, and the art director guessed, as he said, that because of my grandfather (who, in England, had founded a multinational business) I wouldn't be subject to attacks of shyness when meeting the high and mighty.

An early assignment was to photograph the head of Reynolds Metals, in Richmond, Virginia, and his three sons. A stretch limo was sent to meet me at the airport. Thirty minutes later, the driver announced that the "mansion" was in sight. Glinting in the sun, the roof tiles drew my attention. They were aluminum (surely Reynolds aluminum). The house itself was in the colonnaded grand Southern style. The interior was conventionally, traditionally, and overly furnished. Plums, yellows, and reds predominated. Most remarkable was the high-ceilinged Louis XVI drawing room with its two great crystal chandeliers and period furniture. The walls, however, had been entirely papered over in Reynolds aluminum wrap, the shiny stuff you find in your kitchen. It had been partly overlaid with a flocked design, sinuous and oxblood red. The effect, at night when the place was lit with candles, must have been astonishing. In daytime, it was weird.

The three Reynolds sons were cooperative, helpful, and easy to work with. They did what I required of them and showed great patience—attempting to get three people in a single picture to look right requires many exposures. It was George Bernard Shaw, himself interested in photography, who remarked, "The photographer is like the cod, which produces a million eggs in order that one may reach maturity." Even old man Reynolds, father of the three (uniformly short and tubby), didn't make a fuss. But after dinner on the second day, he asked me to follow him into his study.

He sat behind his desk, lit a cigar, leaned back, and spoke:

"Young man, we shall never meet again. You'll leave this house and all you'll remember is money: myself, my three sons, and our money. Appearances are deceptive. Take me, for instance. I'm a poet."

Reynolds père half turned away and, without looking, reached out for a slim, leather-bound book from the shelves in back of the desk. He opened it and started reading a poem he'd written. It was called "The Dollar."

The Dollar addressed you. The Dollar said (in poetic, versified language), I am not evil, I'm a simple Dollar. Just that. The evil is in you people, and, unfairly, you accuse me of corrupting your minds, your manners, and your life. No, I'm only a Dollar. A plain, honest-to-goodness Dollar.

Mr. Reynolds was indeed entirely correct. I remember him today as someone who, beyond worldly achievements, wanted to be thought of as a poet (well, as a would-be poet) rather than as a captain of industry, at the helm of Reynolds Metals and who knows what other planetary ventures.

24

Muhammad Ali

In the spring of 1977 I received a call from Gerry Stutz, president, style-guru, and guiding spirit—the French would call her *une locomotive*—of Henri Bendel, an ultra-smart department store on 57th Street in New York (she later bought the store). She'd seen my portraits of New York businessmen and society women, and she made me an offer: Bendel would set up both a gallery and a studio in the store itself, where chic women could, in great elegance, be photographed. She wanted an exclusivity.

I said no. My work didn't belong in a department store. So far, it had been exhibited in museums and sold in galleries, but William Lieberman, head of drawings at the Museum of Modern Art, said, "Don't be so European. Make some money." The number two at Marlborough Galleries, said of the *locomotive*: "She never makes a mistake. Her instinct never fails her." I gave in.

For Bendel's third floor, I designed a photographic studio and an exhibition space that doubled as a waiting-room. The opening garnered some press fanfare. Eileen Mailey, a top society columnist, wrote a rave piece for her newspaper.

After three weeks and not a single commission, we shut the place down.

Two gentlemen, however, called me for an appointment. One was the baldest man I'd had ever seen, thin, birdlike, and yellowish. The other was an African-American (not the term used in 1977), fleshy and flashy. The portraits at Bendel's were art, they said, "not at all like photographs." They'd been impressed, and they'd come to offer a deal.

The two men were Muhammad Ali's franchisers. Generally, this meant looking for products that could be endorsed by The Greatest. But they also searched for other ways to make money, and here was a case in point. They offered me the franchise of Ali's portraits. A contract, they explained, could be worked out whereby I would own the likeness of Ali, in whatever medium—photography, painting, sculpture— with the exception of press photographs. No one, anywhere, would be able to use or reproduce Ali's portrait without paying me a royalty.

That, as they say, was a license to print money. At the time, Ali was the most famous athlete in the world. Not at the very summit of his career anymore, but still on a pretty elevated plateau—the cynosure of every kid and adolescent in the third world, the flagship of Islam, rich and charismatic. Capital was required, more precisely fifty thousand dollars on the table before anything could happen. A hefty sum at the time, and I approached a friend for help. We each pledged twenty-five thousand. Lawyers moved in, theirs and ours. Contracts were drawn up and submitted to Ali's people in Chicago. Percentages, fees, and bonuses were allotted to everyone connected with the scheme. In the end, however, it was Ali who would decide—Ali who could give or withhold the go-ahead, depending on his mood, on his judgment, and more to the point, how he felt about me. I had to go and call on him in Chicago. I was to be unaccompanied, present myself as an artist, in no way part of a business deal.

Ali lived in a vast, gleaming white, turn-of-the-century mansion on the edge of a mixed white and black neighborhood. I was expected and was immediately led away from a throng of visitors, well-wishers, promoters, panhandlers, seekers of mercy, and business associates who hung around, sitting on the stairs, leaning against walls. I was the only white person.

The living room where I was bidden to wait, alone, was cream and gold, arranged in classical Arab fashion, that is, bare of furniture except for rows of faux Louis XV fauteuils lined up against the walls. At one end of the room stood the largest Sony television set ever made, black and massive, like the Kaaba in Mecca. The floor was covered with a white rug so thick that snowshoes would have eased one's progression across the room. Pulsed air heated the house and blew through a square hole that had been dug out of the white rug, a small well in the centre of the room.

I sat and waited in an armchair for half an hour. At last, the door opened and I was requested to follow a large black man dressed in a white robe. We walked past the people waiting for an audience—there must have been some fifty of them—then down stairways, through corridors, until, in the basement, we arrived at a tall Chinese portico, all red and gold, flanked on one side by a stuffed lion and on the other by a tiger, both standing on all four legs in a growling, menacing stance. In the exercise room beyond the portico, dressed in a blue sports outfit, Ali sat on a low stool and wiped his face with a towel.

I didn't have to introduce myself. Ali had been told. He didn't even look up. I carried with me a large portfolio, which I set down against a wall.

"It's Ramadan," Ali said. "I'm tired. And hungry."

I explained why I was there.

"Show me."

I pulled out the portraits, all of them black-and-white, printed by means of a nineteenth-century method where the blacks are so strong and so matte that the photographs are often mistaken for charcoal drawings.

"Man, that's great drawin'," said Ali.

I explained that they were photographs.

Ali snapped his fingers. Within seconds, a man wearing a beige turban arrived, waiting for instructions. He must have been waiting behind the Chinese portico.

"OK, you can go now," said Ali, and the man disappeared. Then he turned to me with a smile.

"Pretty good, eh?"

I agreed.

Ali once again snapped his fingers, and just as promptly the man returned.

"Get Veronica."

Veronica, his girl of the moment, a tall beauty, red mouth, sleek straightened hair, appeared shortly. We shook hands.

"Gee, they're great drawin's," she said, after a moment's contemplation.

"OK, that's all right, you can go now," Ali told her. Then, turning to me, "She got no education. She thought them were drawin's!"

We worked steadily for three days, mornings only, in a film studio I'd rented in town. Ali always arrived on time, accompanied by friends, handlers, and helpers. He was a real trooper, as they say in the theatre world, and lent himself to all the demands, tricks, and manipulations that a photographer pulls out of his bag. You had to be fast, however, because his attention span was very short, a matter of one minute, after which he got bored and restless. NBC had sent a crew

headed by a producer I knew well. In fact, I was the one who had slipped her the news of the photo session. In no time at all, she took over and tried to turn the situation into a TV program to her liking. I struggled to keep a measure of control. Ali, who in spite of his attention deficiency was acutely intelligent, came to my rescue. "It's John's shoot. If you don't behave yourself, you and your crew are out!"

On the second day, Ali said to me, "I'm not asking you home to lunch. I don't get along with whites."

A devil got into me. "Ali, I don't understand. I've never had that problem."

He cocked his left arm and whacked me on the shoulder. Not hard, but I staggered backwards to keep my balance.

"You're just a little white shit," he said.

But the following day we did have lunch together. Not at home, but at a restaurant. When a couple of weeks later I returned to Chicago with the prints, he inscribed the one I liked best, of his arm extended and his beautiful fist with its well-shaped nails: "To John Stewart, Muhammad Ali, May 13 –77 Love Always."

The scheme fell through, or rather we made no sales. Not one! By contract, the two franchisers were our business managers. The bald man was inept, and the black man alternatively kept polishing his shoes and his nails during business conferences. We tried, my partner and I, to get rid of them, without success. No one wanted posters. No one seemed to want any image of Ali, neither the whites, the Africans, the Muslims, the children, the fans. No one. We lost fifty thousand dollars plus the expenses of lawyers and photography and travel, about seventy-five thousand all told.

Then one day, some six months later, while the one-year contract with Ali was still in force, Andy Warhol called me.

"What's this business?" he asked. "I'm doing a series of portraits of American sports figures, and I'm told I can't do anything with Ali unless I go through you."

I explained the deal to him.

"How much for me to do my number?" he asked.

."Seventy-five thousand dollars."

"You got it."

A few prints of Ali in a drawer are all I have today.

25

About Elephants

Beyond a child's wonderment at the bulk, shape, and accoutrements of the first pachyderm encountered, my earliest singular thought about elephants occurred the day I discovered, in my uncle's library, an elephant's foot turned into a receptacle for four crystal decanters of whiskey. I was fascinated by the immediate presence of the enormous foot, but also angry. You can't say that a small child is "scandalized" but surely that's what I felt. It was a desecration.

Fifteen years later, I found myself working alongside elephants on the infamous Siam-Burma Railway. A number of Japanese engineers and guards had mustered enough English to roar at us, "One erephant same eighty purisona." If only we'd been cared for as well as the elephants! Our distractions were few, and I observed at close quarters the intelligence and the delicacy these animals applied to their tasks. But during *musth*, the rutting season, when at night the female working elephants were tethered to trees in our camp, we would awaken as wild bull elephants came charging out of the jungle in search of mates. The earth shook and trees were knocked down, while we, in our frail palm-thatched huts, wondered whether we would be trampled to death. Yet, of

these nights I also remember keenly a communion with the forest, its wondrous beasts, and their thunderous roaming.

•

The Young Elephant Training Center in Lampang, south of Chiang Mai in Thailand, was an elite school where an elephant student would only be admitted if its mother worked for the Thai Department of Forestry. I wanted to write and illustrate a children's book about the school,* and I went to see the director of the Elephant Work Force to obtain the necessary authorization.

* *Elephant School*, Pantheon, New York, 1982.

In the course of travels in Kenya, Uganda, and Tanzania, I'd observed African elephants in the wilds, and I put to the director, a trained veterinarian, a question which had troubled me: Why was it possible to train Asian elephants (*Elephas maximus*) to perform complicated tasks, to understand orders, seemingly to domesticate them, when, as far as I knew, no such thing was possible with *Loxodonta africana*. The director's explanation was unconvincing: "There's a canal in the elephant's brain. Although the Asian elephant is smaller in size than the African, his canal is wider, allowing ideas to flow more freely." The director unknowingly echoed the antique Asian judgment concerning *Loxodonta*, "in intelligence and work training retarded and slow."

Was it once more a question of nature or nurture? Were Asian mahouts more skillful than their African counterparts (if the latter existed at all)? Or had nature favored *maximus* for intelligence and *Loxodonta* for size? I decided to find out.

Nothing is known about the training of North African elephants two thousand years ago, but something can be learned from the attempts to train the larger Central African breed in the nineteenth and twentieth centuries.*

Having observed the performance of elephants in Ceylon, King Leopold II of Belgium decided to use the enormous pool of pachyderms available in the Congo, his own private possession. In 1879, two male and two female elephants were purchased in India and shipped to Dar es Salaam, along with fourteen mahouts. At Leopold's request, the British consul in Baghdad took command of the expedition—a very large one, 700 soldiers, servants, and camp followers. The caravan provoked astonishment among the tribes who claimed that white

---

* John Stewart, "The Elephant in War," *The Quarterly Journal of Military History*, New York, Spring 1991.

gods were on their way, and that "elephants carry loads like donkeys." Five months later, only one elephant, Pulmalla, had survived the journey. In the Congo, she became a great favorite among her black handlers, much spoiled and fussed over. But when the consul left the Congo, accompanied by a British friend who had joined him for the return journey, Pulmalla became grief-stricken, refused all food, and died. Then there was more bad news: along the way, the two Englishmen were ambushed and murdered.

Undeterred, Leopold ordered the establishment of a jungle depot where elephants could be trained after their capture. Commandant Laplume was put in charge of the project, and the village of Kira-Vanga, in the Bas Uli district of the Congo, now the Central African Republic, was selected as the base because of the great herds of elephants that roamed the forest. Methods of capture and training were modeled on those used in South East Asia. Only kindness was tolerated, and anyone who broke that rule was punished. If an elephant killed its trainer after being badly treated, no action was taken: the animal was within its right.

The project was only moderately successful. In 1938 there were eighty-four elephants trained for timberwork, a low figure considering all the time and effort expended. Nor did their performance equal that of the Indian elephants. The question then remains. Were the African handlers less skillful than the Indian mahouts, or is *Loxodonta* effectively less gifted than its Asian cousin?*

This brings up another debate, the one concerning Hannibal's elephants. Considerable evidence indicates they were

---

* A 2007 doctorate thesis by Fanny D. M. Cohen states that *Loxodonta* can be trained almost to the levels attained by *Elephas*, although it will take more time and effort. *Loxodonta*, however, cannot walk upright on his hind legs.

African. Carthaginian coins clearly show the specific head and ears of *Loxodonta africana*. If so, how did Hannibal train them and lead them across the Rhône and the Alpine passes, and how were they taught the necessary fighting skills? The Carthaginian elephants didn't originate in Central Africa. Taxonomically, they're a subspecies classed as *Loxodonta africana cyclotis*, and they lived in the forests of North Africa, isolated from the rest of the continent by the Sahara desert. They figure in bas-reliefs found at the Bardo Museum, close to Tunis. Interestingly, the size of their handlers would indicate that they're smaller than their *Africana* cousins. By the end of the second century A.D. they were extinct except in the mountains of the High Atlas, where they survived until the arrival of the Arabs.

The supposition concerning Hannibal's elephants is confirmed by the accounts of the Battle of Raphia (a town now in the Gaza Strip) in 217 B.C., the only recorded event in which *Loxodonta* faced *Elephas*. The encounter was so extraordinary that the foot soldiers of both camps called a temporary truce simply to watch the contest. *Elephas* won easily. Three historians, Polybius, Pliny, and Diodorus, write that African elephants were smaller, weaker, and less courageous than their opponents. And here surely is the clue: those African elephants must have been the North African variety, not as tall as *Elephas*, in turn smaller than *Loxodonta*.

For a moment, I was tempted to communicate my findings to the director of the Elephant Work Force in Bangkok, but discretion being the better part of valor, I did nothing. I don't think it would have changed his anatomical beliefs.

26

The Butterfly Chair

Summer weekends, if I'd worked hard enough to deserve it, I hired a small plane equipped with floats to fly me to Fire Island. It took off from the East River in midtown Manhattan, slipped under the 59th Street Bridge, and half an hour later deposited me on the Great South Bay, that body of water between Long Island and Fire Island, only a stone's throw away from my house.

Fire Island is merely a strip of sand, parallel to Long Island, thirty-five miles long and about five hundred yards at its widest. The beach is vast, unending, enticing. Sea grass grows on the sand dunes, and a sunken forest of holly, pitch pine, and bayberry runs along the center of the island, below sea level. My wife and our small son would be waiting for me at the wooden pier, and we followed the boardwalk to our house sitting on stilts atop a dune, facing the Atlantic. There were no cars, no electricity, no billboards, no crowds.

George Balanchine and Tanaquil Le Clercq came for a weekend in August 1956. Tanaquil was the prima ballerina of the New York City Ballet and Balanchine's fourth wife. She was twenty-seven and they'd been married for three years. She was beautiful, with the longest legs imaginable and sinuous, elegant body lines. "Mona Lisa as a *Vogue* model," it was said of her. Balanchine, one of the greatest choreographers of the twentieth century, had taken the New York City Ballet to its heights and to its fame.

The morning after their arrival, Tanaquil and I went walking on the beach while Balanchine and my Russian wife stayed in the house, talking and drinking tea. The air was salty and bracing, the Atlantic Ocean was in a quiet mood, and the sun shed a soft light. The morning was still young. We walked at a good pace on the hardened wet sand or else splashed through the foam. We hardly said a word. It was one of those moments when you thought, "There's nowhere in the world where I'd rather be just now than here." Gentle waves were breaking on the sand, bringing driftwood and kelp and the remains of soft shell crabs that looked so primitive that evolution seemed to have passed them by. And then, emerging from the foam, we came across a rattan armchair, one of these huge armchairs with wings, known as butterfly chairs and made in the Philippines. A wreck standing askew above the water, like a sloop marooned on a sandbank, swaying gently as waves broke around it. Tanaquil turned to me, smiled, and took off at a run, her long legs striding and glinting in the sun. She soared over the chair and I swear she appeared to stop above it for an instant. She floated down rather than hit the water, turned around and, once more, did *le grand écart*, an apparition in the scintillating sky. I wailed in despair, "Tanaquil, I don't have a camera!" But she had one back at the house, a Leica, loaded with film. As I went to retrieve it, I thought of Nijinsky, who when asked how he managed to stop in mid-air, as Tanaquil had done, said (these are not his exact words), "I rise and then I stop. It's that simple." Balanchine gave me the Leica, an old-fashioned model, I ran down the dune, rejoined Tanaquil, and shot the whole roll of black-and-white film at one thousandth of a second.

Back to New York on Monday, I handed the roll of film over to Ernst, my German darkroom assistant. It was the record of an exceptional situation, I told him, and he was to develop it by inspection because, on the beach, without a light meter, I'd had to guess the exposure. Ten minutes later, Ernst came out, the film still dripping wet in hand. The exposure was correct, but of the image there was nothing but rectangular, dark grey blurs. I suddenly understood my mistake. The ancient Leica's lens was retractable, and I'd failed to recognize it as such. I hadn't pulled it out of its housing, and the images were hopelessly out-of-focus.

That fall, the New York City Ballet went off on a European tour. By November they were in Copenhagen where Tanaquil fell ill. It was polio. She was paralyzed from the waist down, never recovered the use of her legs, and spent the rest of her life in a wheelchair. She died, at age seventy-one, on December 31, 2000.

Tanaquil had been fourteen in 1944 when Balanchine first approached her. He had choreographed a ballet to Mozart's music for the March of Dimes, an American charitable organization that assisted polio victims and financed polio research in America. Tanaquil danced the lead part in a performance at the Waldorf-Astoria Hotel. Clive Barnes, writing an obituary, "Elegy for Tanny," in *Dance Magazine*, described that performance:

> A classroom of ballet girls practiced classic steps until a monster in black, danced by Balanchine himself, intruded on the scene, touching and paralyzing one of the students. The girl was the 14-year-old Tanny, and Balanchine, of course, was supposed to be Polio. As she sat paralyzed in a chair, people threw silver coins at her until, miraculously, she rose and danced again.

27

Amdo

Sighing and creaking, the Toyota rambles on from deep rut to mud hole. The front end settles down with a dull crack and the car climbs out with a groan. A torrent roars just below the road. Deafened and shaken, there's no point in attempting any form of conversation. Anyway, all five of us are cooped up in that autistic reverie proper to long car trips.

"Quick, take a look. We're in Tibet!" Anthony's voice, heard through the racket.

We move over to his side, noses against the mud-spattered windows. On the far bank of the creek, a cluster of white banners flying on tall poles stands at the edge of a dark wood. A Buddhist grove.

"Bye bye China!"

Further on, like a clip from a Kurosawa film, close formations of banners emerge over the ridge of a hill, follow the contours of a valley, and march across fields, scattering their mantras to the wind.

"Every year, every Buddhist brings one flag," announces Jigme.

A few hundred feet off the road, a line of tents spreads out at the foot of a hill. Or rather the ghosts of tents. Mere skeletons, lacy, transparent, and without substance, they look like a gigantic cat's-cradle gone wrong, an entanglement of poles and spars joined by a network of lines from which hang hundreds of tattered prayer flags. These airy mazes, ruined by the rain and bleached by the sun, incessantly whipped by the wind, stand far from any human dwelling—votary structures, gratuitous follies, inhabited by the spirits of Bön, the old shamanistic cult of the Tibetan regions.

Inside the labyrinth, like a fly caught in a spider's web, I struggle with wide-angle lenses.

"Tibet lives!" booms Anthony. The words fly off in the turbulent air. The flags quiver. The rain comes down once more. Hunched under the icy wetness, we race back to the Toyota.

We were in the Grasslands, the high altitude steppes on the border of China and Tibet, slap in the middle of the rainy season. It was July, nominally summer, but the saying about this part of the world is that it knows only one season: winter. Rain turned to hail, sleet to snow, drizzle to fog. Rocketing down from Mongolia, a freezing wind whipped the hills. Yet, moments later, the cloud cover ripped open, revealing strips of translucent and preternaturally blue sky. Like the death rays in a comic strip, crystalline shafts of sun set grass and wild flowers afire with color. For a brief moment, the snowy peaks of the Anyemaqen Range, two hundred miles to the northwest, ringed the edge of the enormous sky.

The black clouds gathered once more, their shadows skimming over the undulating steppe. The sun was obscured. "And darkness was upon the face of the deep," quoted Anthony, digging back to his Scottish Presbyterian childhood.

We were five on this mad trip to a country strictly closed to foreigners: Anthony, a publisher of books on Tibet, and Marie-Laure, his French wife; Heather, who spoke Tibetan and lived in Paris with her husband, a lama from Amdo;

Jigme, a Tibetan cousin of the lama, who also spoke Mandarin and English; and myself. We'd hired the Toyota and its driver in Chengdu, close to the border, and told him to drive in a westerly direction—until he realized he'd taken us into forbidden territory. We reassured him that whatever happened we'd take the blame. He beamed. "This is wonderful, for the first time I meet foreigners, and for the first time I break the law!" Daily, as we moved from one place to another, we were stopped by police and army. Our presence was both incomprehensible and intolerable. We told them we were all related, all one family, on our way to visit our Chinese in-laws (in truth Heather's Tibetan in-laws). The effect of surprise coupled with the enormity of the story worked wonders. We were neither expelled nor sent to prison.

Amdo, beyond the Great Wall, has always been a sensitive border region, with a tumultuous history. It's the nomads' home ground—a fierce lot, as fierce as their mastiffs, and they resist the unrelenting Chinese pressure to impose on them the Han way of life. I'm sure they're still doing so, although this is a story that took place in the summer of 1988.

The Amdo Beggar

At mealtimes in the Grasslands, the talk was about Buddhism, the black yaks and the black tents, the filth of our dreadful inn and its revolting latrines, the incessant rain, and the ways of the Tibetan nomads. We were seated at our favorite restaurant in Labrang, an ancient town of Amdo.

Chinese Moslems, or Huis, ran the restaurant. The food was good, infinitely better than Tibetan fare and different from Han. The place was not only our canteen but also my studio. Its whitewashed walls, the bare earth floor, and the rough unpainted beams that supported the ceiling, provided an unobtrusive background. And a large window facing north shed a soft and yet directional light. This is where I induced people I met on the streets and in the markets—monks and nuns, itinerant sellers, schoolboys and horsemen—to come and sit for me. My friends couldn't understand why I didn't photograph people wherever they happened to be, rather than bother them to come all the way to my "studio." Photojournalism has never had a great appeal for me. I favor the private world of the studio, its space, the isolation it offers, and the control it provides in both lighting and composition.

No Amdoan—Chinese, Hui, or Tibetan—ever failed to appear, nor did anyone ask to be recompensed or even request a print. The exception was a Bön shaman who not only was vain—he would not be photographed with his wonderful old-fashioned Chinese eyeglasses—but requested the immediate delivery of thirty prints of himself for distribution to his flock. Amdo, in brief, appeared to be one of these exceptional places on the globe where *homo photographans* is not only tolerated but actively sought, where people jostle one another to make sure they are caught by the lens.

At lunchtime one day, seated at our regular table close to a window, I heard a woman's voice. I turned around, but saw only a hand stretched in through the window, an open hand asking for alms. Having no loose change, I impulsively took my bowl of *tupa*, our daily fare of mutton and noodles, and deposited it in the open hand. A woman's face then appeared in the window, a face that showed neither surprise nor pleasure. The eyes, however, met mine as if a flow of understanding coursed between this woman and me. Not the look that questions, but the look of recognition. Had giving her my food, rather than dropping a coin in her hand, bridged the incalculable gap between our lives? We had met. It was that simple. Such were the thoughts that struck me at the time.

I indicated to one of the Chinese waiters standing by that he should go bring her in. He knew my routine. She entered the restaurant—a woman in her late thirties, in her forties perhaps, it was hard to say—and without a moment's hesitation she came toward me. She wasn't alone. A moon-faced boy, surely her son, held the pinky of her right hand, and in her left she held my bowl of *tupa*. An old woman, a dwarf, hobbling on a cane followed them. All three wore ragged and filthy clothes. I motioned them to stand in front of the wall. The woman, still holding the bowl level with her face, now smiled, a smile full of silence, the smile, it struck me at the time, of a woman who has pleased her man, who herself has been pleasured. She looked at me brazenly, standing proud. The boy, sucking a stick he held in his hand, stared away from the camera, mouth open. The dwarf, leaning on her cane, faced me, head cocked to the side, inscrutable. I brought the camera to my eye. There was nothing to do, nothing to change, a perfect arrangement. I clicked the shutter. Once only, because as if by a secret understanding, as if by a trick of collective consciousness, all three instantly turned away and made for the door, the woman still grasping my lunch bowl in her hand.

•

This need of ours, humans, to maintain our internal furnace at a constant thirty-seven degrees Celsius—the reason why, unlike reptiles, we have to eat thrice daily—has had strange consequences. Unlike sex, when most of us seek privacy *à deux*, food is characterized by its social aspect. We like to assemble with members of our species to share our food, to break bread. True, many species eat together, but they do so only with their immediate kin: a lion walking in the savannah and who runs across another lion will not invite him to come and share a bone. Once, as I was flying with a few friends over the Rift Valley in East Africa we spotted Richard Leakey's base camp and its landing strip. By radio, we requested permission to land. Leakey suggested we might be interested to see his recent digs, and he handed us over to one his African helpers. Most excavations of that kind don't reveal much to the uninitiated eye. We were shown a couple of skulls that might have belonged to primates. Yet, said our guide, they could well have belonged to hominids. Back at the base, Leaky explained that buried around these remains they had found the bones of animals, no doubt killed for food. A reason, the only one, to surmise that here lived hominids rather than primates—our remote ancestors, like us, assembled to share their food.

Food is magic. Its gross substance transforms itself into our immaterial thoughts and emotions, and magic requires ritual. This recalls a strange episode recounted by Norbert Elias in *The Civilizing Process*. A Byzantine princess invited to a Venetian state dinner in the seventeenth century, helped herself to food from the communal platter using a gold fork she had brought with her. Like everyone else, she should have used her hand. Such was the indignation caused by her refusal to partake in what was perceived as a form of communion, that excommunication was contemplated. She'd committed a sacrilege. However, whether for political or other reasons, excommunication was ruled out. When the bubonic plague hit Venice a few years later, everyone knew it was God's punishment for having failed to excommunicate the princess.

Pandas

Ten miles before reaching the Jiuzhaigou Reserve, we stopped at a hut by the roadside to pay our entrance fee. Our driver Xiang Fu, and Jigme, both Chinese citizens, were charged half a yuan each, twenty-five cents in US dollars. For Overseas Chinese the fee is doubled. "Friends," like us, are dunned three yuans "to show the extent of our friendship."

The valley narrowed. We went by a few hamlets, neat houses and well-tended gardens. Jigme was indignant. This was Bönpo territory. Twelfth-century texts show that this part of the region was neither a vassal of China nor of Tibet. How dare the recent Chinese immigrants install themselves in this ancient land? Further on, Jigme asked us to halt. He pointed out small blue flowers peeking above the grass, aconites whose white, bulbous root contains a powerful poison. The Khampas, he explained, the last guerrillas to fight the Chinese, use it to commit suicide rather than fall into PLA hands and face torture.

The Jiuzhaigou Reserve was a Giant Panda habitat. The Giant Panda is the emblematic beast of China, but its numbers are fast decreasing, and outside of zoos, it might eventually be found only in reserves. Up in the hills, the bamboo was red and droopy—dead or dying. Mountain bamboo blooms every fifty or sixty years. After this apotheosis the roots blacken and the plant dies. The seeds then fall to the ground and germinate. Fifteen years later they have grown into thickets that provide, once again, the pandas' sustenance. Unless the animals travel to another live bamboo territory (not all stands of bamboo flourish simultaneously), they perish. But these feeding grounds are distant, often unreachable or else given over to cultivation. If as a species the pandas disappear, the cause will not have been entirely man's fault. Because of their notoriously inefficient and ill-adapted digestive system, pandas assimilate only a small portion of what they eat, and they eat nothing but bamboo.

A story published in the local paper tells of the peasant woman who was cutting wood by a riverbank when she spotted a Giant Panda floating downstream. She threw her-self into the icy waters and dragged the beast ashore. With local people's help, it was hauled up the bank. A fire was lit. When it came out of its frozen torpor, the panda leaped up a tree and would not be coaxed down. The peasants offered it smoked meat, maize porridge, and cakes. Not surprisingly, the panda wasn't tempted and remained where it was until the local "Panda Rescue Team" arrived. The story ends well: After a short stay in hospital, the beautiful bear is now living happily in a zoo.

The lodge was a well-designed, one-story building set on the edge of a bluff, overlooking a vast expanse of hills and forests. The site was perfect, and the weather had turned sunny, almost warm. The sordid Chinese-built townships were distant, and we were in an expansive mood, but it didn't last. Rock-and-roll was booming from a yellow bus parked at the entrance to the lodge. Forty Hong Kong teenagers were touring Amdo. Prey to a collective hyperactivity, they were unloading their stridently colored gear and throwing on the ground empty Marlboro packs, candy wrappers, soiled tis-sues, and empty soda-pop cans, along with that worldwide spoor of the tourist of pre-digital days, the black-and-yellow Kodak film box. I suggested to Anthony that we go and put a stop to this barbaric behavior.

"Where you from?" asked a sharp-looking boy wearing tinted glasses.

"We from Soviet Union," said Anthony. The accent was totally believable.

"In Rossia, go to prison for throwing rubbish," I added, getting into the act.

A pretty girl joined in. "At home in Hong Kong, we never do this."

"So why here? This not home?" I asked.

Anthony got into this routine whenever he contemplated an impressive landscape: a wide sweep of the arm and the famous Little Lord Fauntleroy quote, "Do you know that some day it will all belong to you?" In this instance the quote turned into, "But one day all this your country."

The teenagers were crowding around us, doubting, questioning. We assured them that littering would take them straight to a Siberian gulag. As we walked away, I delivered the coup de grâce: "We're not Russian, you creeps! We're British. And you're a bunch of messy Chinese!" Mixed roars of pain, rage, and also laughter.

All the rooms and dormitories were occupied by the teenagers, and the lodge-keeper offered to put us up in his house up the hill. He was emphatic. It was his own, and not the reserve's. We moved in. It was scrupulously clean, the wooden floors and walls were wonderfully fragrant, and the view on all sides incomparable.

From the verandah, the lodge-keeper pointed out a large tree in the middle distance. Some months ago, he'd witnessed an arboreal combat between two Giant Pandas fighting for the attention of a female who sat at the foot of the tree, awaiting the outcome. After a particularly ferocious bout, both males fell off a high branch and were killed, leaving the would-be widow to look for another mate.

We didn't see any pandas. We saw hundreds of silvery waterfalls tumbling down the mountain until they formed translucent pools. Fingers of white water slipped around trees, merging into sinuous labyrinths forming, further down, small turquoise lakes bursting with aquatic ferns and flowers. Breaking through the feathery trees, shafts of sun played over the waters in ever-changing patterns.

A log bridge led across a torrent to an island of verdant and airy lushness. I laid myself out in the grass amid the primula, the edelweiss, and the wild strawberries, lulled by the torrent's rush and gurgle, observing lazy, fleecy clouds slowly sailing in the sky. The stream purred like a cat, and a delicious languor overwhelmed me.

Gedün Chöpel

The grasslands are behind us. That part of the journey is over. We've left the nomads, the black tents, the yaks and the mastiffs, the green hills and the rain. We're on our way to the birthplace of a man whose story we've heard from Heather.

Gedün Chöpel was born in Amdo, and very early in life showed an exceptional propensity for independent thinking. Everyone noted a wild streak and a strong-willed character. Maintaining the heretical view that plants have a soul, he was expelled from his monastery. He also believed that it was necessary to descend to the depths in order to reach the heights, and for.a while he led a life of debauchery in India. Eager for reform, he joined a dissident Amdoan group that opposed some of Lhasa's policies. The Chinese got wind of it. Through their agents, they leaked out to Lhasa a piece of disinformation with disastrous consequences for Tibet: They revealed that Gedün Chöpel was planning an Amdo separatist movement. He was arrested. He defended himself, it was all lies. The truth was that the Chinese were about to invade. No one believed him. He was thrown in prison, his library was sacked. After his release and his rehabilitation in 1951, he died, at age forty-six, a victim of alcohol and tobacco.

We followed an unpaved road, little better than a track, toward the village where Gedün Chöpel's family now lives, through a gorge opening onto a lush valley—the valley of the White Eagle. This was the Repkong district, the northeastern part of Amdo. The village has electricity and a telephone line, but set amid red cliffs it looks like a troglodyte settlement. Bales of hay were heaped atop tall and strange wooden structures. I first believed them to have a totemic function, then thought they'd serve as an admirable installation of contemporary art, and finally settled for a pragmatic explanation: The hay was placed up there to dry. We were directed to a house. The door was locked. We knocked at the neighbor's. They asked us to enter, and offered us tea and the most excellent bread. Presently, the late monk's family arrived, with an old woman, a cousin of Gedün Chöpel, deeply stooped, advancing painfully with the help of a relative. When she heard why we had come to visit, she let out a few sobs through her clenched teeth. She had lockjaw. We talked about Gedün, his life, the injustice he suffered, and the great sadness of his death.

The old cousin managed a few words through her frozen mouth. Her relative made them clear: "The terrible thing is that Gedün has not reincarnated. The Emperor, these days, does not allow anyone to reincarnate."

We must meet the mayor. A young man climbs on the roof of the house, and after much shouting, comes down, and we're assured that the mayor, who is now attending a meeting, will soon join us. Marigolds, mustard, and golden stalks of barley grow on the flat roof, ruffled by the wind. White butterflies by the hundreds scamper among the flowers. The sun is hot.

The mayor arrives, and we move next door, to the family house. The mayor is a man in his late thirties, with a strong face. He barks an oratory of welcome, ending with a request for names, ages, and nationalities. After the inevitable scribbling, we can get down to normal conversation, in a normal tone of voice. The mayor would rather we moved to the Commune's house, so we all troop to the village, down tortuous and precipitous paths. The Commune's house has become the district office. The only sign of the Chinese presence is a plaster bas-relief of Mao, about two inches in diameter, hung discreetly out of the way. The mayor's opinion of world affairs is that technologically Tibet is two hundred years behind the West. In other ways it need not fear comparison with any other country. He is proud of being Tibetan, he says. As head of all the villages in the vicinity, he has, no doubt, been vetted and put in place by the Chinese. He speaks Mandarin fluently. He is the new breed of Tibetan, born after the invasion of 1950. Both the Chinese and the Tibetans can trust him.

The door opens and we meet the schoolmaster, also a Tibetan, but much older than the mayor. The white ceremonial scarves, the *kathas*, are exchanged. He has brought us a basket of apples. A hundred children are in his care, and Tibet, its language, and its culture, comes before China. His ambition is to establish a Gedün Chöpel cultural center in the village. He is confident that Lhasa will release his writings. We take our leave. We shake hands. They thank us for coming, and wish us to return three more times, at ten-year intervals. The mayor promises big changes.

As we leave the valley, a white eagle hovers high above us, suddenly wheels away and drops out of sight.

28

Shooting a Leopard

That evening, the General's stride was slower than usual. He slumped down in a rattan chair and lit a cigarette.

"Had a good day?" he asked.

"Bad," I replied. "Just hanging around."

"Same here. Can't go on like this, bugger all to do."

We shared an attap-roofed hut, the General and I, with a Tamil manservant to attend our needs. The hut was set under the jungle canopy close to the river where *The Bridge on the River Kwai* was being filmed. We'd been appointed technical advisers, drawing scandalously high salaries but, as it turned out, with hardly anything to do. It sounds like an idyllic set-up, but we were bored. David Lean, the movie's director, had no need of us. He wasn't interested. Once I pointed out to him that a bunch of extras in the roles of POWs were filmed dragging a heavy tree trunk up hill, away from the bridge—an absurd situation. The reaction was swift: "It looks as if they're working harder, and please leave me alone." As for General Perowne, his contribution (one time only) was to parade the extras in military rows of fours, a task equally suited to a retired corporal.

We changed for dinner and joined the director's table. After the second course, during a lull in the conversation, the General turned to David Lean.

"I say, David, do you need John and me for the next fortnight or so?"

"Not particularly, General," said David.

"Very well then. We'll be off at dawn. And, incidentally, we'd like to draw a Land Rover from the motor-pool."

I never found out how the General had been discovered by Sam Spiegel, the film producer, but with me it started one day at breakfast when my wife pointed out a short piece in the *New York Times* about Spiegel acquiring the rights to Pierre Boulle's book with its eponymous title. By eleven I was in Spiegel's office, showing him a sketch of the Sonkrai bridge that I'd drawn on the back of a Japanese roll-call form. The two-tiered bridged spanned the Kwai, and as I've said, I'd worked on it when I was a prisoner in Thailand. I also mentioned in an off-hand manner that I spoke Japanese, had been one of the few interpreters, hence well acquainted with the mentality and the behavior of our captors. I also let it be known (pure anticipation) that *Life* magazine had asked me to cover the film—both text and pictures. With such offerings, Sam had to sign me up on the spot as technical adviser. I left him, trotted over to the offices of *Life*, a few blocks away, and instantly received an assignment to cover the story—both text and pictures.

As for Lancelot Perowne, he is best described using British military clichés, as ramrod stiff, lean as a whippet, bristling red moustache. His rank was that of Brigadier-General, lowest grade of generalship, which he attributed to the poor opinion he had held of the men under his command. He had no doubt about them—in civilian life, they wore pointed blue suede shoes. His contempt, he suspected, had became apparent and blocked his promotion.

Perowne lived in a village called Hurtmore Bottom. While his wife was at church on Sunday mornings, he sat at his desk, field glasses at hand, and from a window kept watch for anyone trespassing on his property. On the desk, a set of imaginary buttons controlled machine guns positioned in a fold of the land or hidden in a copse. Whenever he saw an unauthorized person walking across his fields, he'd wipe them out by pressing the button that corresponded to the strategically placed imaginary machine gun.

•

We motored through Ceylon (as Sri Lanka was then known), and I thought it was the most wondrous and luminous country I'd seen in all my travels. At the top of Adam's Peak, the highest mountain in Ceylon, a rock carries the imprint of a human foot, but about fifty inches long. According to one's belief, it's Buddha's, Muhammad's, or Adam's foot. The pilgrims of all three faiths climb the mountain in the course of one day and one night. We did it in one short night, supposedly to avoid the heat of the day. In fact, I think Perowne needed a challenge.

The path was steep. Perowne climbed indefatigably, always ahead. If ever I stopped at spots celebrating incidents that had occurred in the course of the holy men's ascent, he would say, "No time for lingering." Passing some thorny bushes, for instance, where the Buddha (or Muhammad or Adam) caught his robe, it's traditional to deposit needle and thread. The bushes have the appearance of huge white cocoons. Not carrying the requisite offering, I asked one of the pilgrims if he had it to spare. "No time for such things," the General said sternly.

Two-thirds of the way up the peak, close to collapse, I slumped down on a stone step, urging Perowne to continue without me. I'd wait there and join him later. I then learned that not only did he look the part, but that he also embodied the characteristics of generalship. His words carried simultaneously both threat and compassion. I knew that unless I got up and followed him, I would carry the shame of this weakness throughout my life. In brief, I had to obey my superior officer even it meant heart failure. I scrambled to my feet and with renewed vigor completed the climb. Perowne was a leader.

Shortly after we reached the summit, the sun rose and threw the mountain's shadow—a giant triangle—over the jungle all the way down to the sea. Below in the forest, wild elephants trumpeted. The sky turned grey-pink. Then, due to an extraordinary phenomenon of refraction, the shadow disappeared and reappeared two more times. The pilgrims chanted. We hit a large bell just once to tell the gods it was our first pilgrimage, and then we left.

A week later, after the green hills and the tea gardens, we were traveling north through tropical forest. By late afternoon we stopped to ask indications of an infantry platoon of the Sinhalese Army, twenty men commanded by a sergeant. Had they heard if the English Rest House shown on the maps was still operative? It was, we were told, and located fifteen miles down the road. We were offered tea, Perowne asked the questions that a general would ask, and everyone was friendly.

The rest house, like hundreds of others, had been set up in the days of the Raj to shelter officials in the course of their journeys. In these bungalows, one would find a primitive shower, an Indian bed of wood and rope, known as a *charpoy*, a mosquito net, a rice-and-chicken curry, and sometimes a beer. And that is precisely what awaited us.

It was still dark when we were awakened by the sound of voices outside our window. We got up and learned that a leopard had entered a village house and taken a baby. There was no adequate gun in the village, but surely we had one, and would we go and shoot the leopard. The villagers would act as trackers. Whatever remained of the child, it had to receive a decent burial. But we had no weapons.

"Let's go and see the Sinhalese Rifles down the road," said Perowne. We went off, driving fast through the dawn.

The sentry on duty was told to get the sergeant. We explained why we needed to borrow a couple of rifles along with a half-dozen rounds, noses filed down to turn them into dumdum bullets. "No problem," said the sergeant, recognizing, as I had at Adam's Peak, the General's authority. Handing weapons over to civilians is of course an offense of extreme gravity, but this was nothing less than a categorical imperative, a situation that wasn't negotiable. We'd talked about the bullets on the way over: military ammunition has sharp tips, and a round would fail to stop a charging animal—it would go right through its body. A flat-nose bullet (known as a dumdum) would arrest the charge. We were handed two Lee-Enfield rifles and six 303 rounds suitably altered.

Back at the village half a dozen men—our trackers—were waiting. Following broken twigs, trampled grass, and at one spot traces of blood, they led us across cultivated fields into the jungle. A gentle breeze blew toward us: our scent wouldn't carry, and we had a good chance of surprising the leopard. The path narrowed and the going slowed down. I was in the lead, cradling the heavy Lee-Enfield, a familiar weight, since it was my first weapon in the British Army. I had two dumdum rounds in the magazine and one in the breech. Perowne was just behind me. No one spoke.

The path debouched onto a small clearing. The head tracker stopped short like a gun dog. So did I. With an almost imperceptible motion of his right hand, the tracker indicated that I was to take a step forward. The leopard was in the

shadows. Crouching, head low, the remains of the baby between its paws. As he heard us, his head came up. His yellow gaze locked onto my eyes. For an instant, we were both motionless, paralyzed by the inevitability of the situation, tensing for the preordained moment. I raised my rifle and slowly squeezed the trigger. I was ready to take the recoil and above my sights I saw the leopard make a small jump and then slump down as if it had gone to sleep. There was no need to check if he was dead. The round had gone right through the head, above the eyes, leaving a large and ragged hole. Dumdum bullets are terribly destructive and banned for military use by international law.

The villagers crowded around the carcass. Perowne and I stayed away. They thanked us, and asked me if I wanted the pelt. I said yes, and they requested permission to take away the muscles of the neck. When I asked why, the answer surprised me: "Our people in the village have asthma. If they eat the neck muscles, they feel better."

They skinned the leopard on the spot, and back at the village the pelt was scraped clean, smeared with ashes, rolled up in a jute bag, and handed over to me.

A month later in Kandy, the capital, I met a local doctor and asked him if he had an explanation for the villagers' strange request.

"Simple," he said. "All mammals under stress, including man of course, produce adrenaline from two glands situated above the kidneys. Adrenaline, a neurotransmitter, travels to the brain through the blood in the neck muscles, and produces the necessary reactions for dealing with the situation. Adrenaline is also a specific for asthma."

By the time I returned to New York, small ticks had eaten holes in the leopard pelt. I'd had it properly cured in Kandy, but apparently to no effect. There was just enough left to cover two cushions. The cushions followed my family's peregrination from America to Switzerland and then back to America. Eventually they became brittle, the skin split, and they had to be disposed of. Anyway, the time would soon have come when having two leopard cushions on the sofa would have been politically incorrect, or rather, ecologically unacceptable.

29

Fayum

"**O**pen it," said my father. "Your godfather—he was an Egyptologist, remember?—gave it to me in Cairo, eons ago."

The thin waxed cord was as stiff as wire, and the knot was so tight that I had to cut it; the wrapping, an Arabic newspaper, was so brittle that it broke apart when I tried to unfold it. I held in my hands the image of a boy, a portrait painted on wood. A smoky, vaporous figure, which appeared to sink into its dark background, the eyes fixed in a distant gaze, yet present, insistent and glazed with mystery. "Copt, I think, first century A.D.," added my father as an afterthought. It had to be mine. Here was a need unrelated to the collector's greed or the aesthete's passion, not even to the fleeting thought that it might have been meant to be mine and had rested for over thirty years in the drawer I had inadvertently pulled open. It was, in brief, both the shock of discovery and that of recognition . . .

My father agreed that I could have it. Like a Russian family icon, the Fayum Boy has followed me in all my abodes, houses, lodgings, and apartments, in America and Europe.

The Fayum is a Nile region where lived a Greek minority, and the "mysterious portraits" as they're often referred to were produced from the first to the fourth century. Although funerary, they were executed during the lifetime of the subject. They're striking, and the vividness of their colors is due to the techniques used—encaustic and egg tempera. The faces are mostly Egyptian, the prevalent type and the dominant culture, with the admixture of Greece and Rome. Closer to our time, it must have been the equivalent to the Levantine world, that unique and rich mix of Arab, Greek, Italian, French, English, and Jewish cultures that disappeared with the onset of the Second World War.

My plaque was typical of many Fayum portraits: five slats of polished wood, the whole measuring eight by thirteen inches. I took it to a prominent Florentine framer in New York, where I was then living. We chose a Baroque frame, deeply chiseled and flecked with a gold impasto. For background to the plaque, we picked a creamy velvet with a soft yellow hue. The effect was sumptuous and yet restrained.

There was, however, an aspect of my Fayum Boy that was singular: it was, as I've said, evanescent, as if emerging from a mist, utterly discreet in coloring. A mysterious rendering, as if the artist had wished to question the untimely death of a young and beautiful human being—the opposite of the classical, forceful, high-in-color Fayum portrait. I consulted several books but never saw any reproduction that approached the style of my own portrait.

Over the years, from my carriage house in New York it moved to a Swiss chalet, thence to a Paris apartment and my photographic studio. It was high time to get an expert opinion. I had to find out what lay behind the singularity of the Fayum Boy. A French collector of Egyptian antiquities asked me to meet him at his regular restaurant. I'd taken the Fayum out of its frame. The collector gave it a glance. "Rub-

bish," was all he said, and called for the menu. He wouldn't elaborate, "not worthwhile," but discussed minutely the day's special with the headwaiter.

I made an appointment with the curator of Egyptian antiquities at the Louvre, and was put in touch with an ecclesiastic, a specialist in Fayum. He looked at my plaque for a long while and turned to me with a smile. "It's exceptional, a rare piece, the perfect link between Egyptian and Greek art. I've been looking for it for a long time." He wanted me to give it or at least lend it to the museum. I said I'd think it over, knowing full well that there was no possibility of letting it go anywhere.

I moved to London. An exhibition of Fayum portraits was due to open at the British Museum. I obtained an appointment with the curator of the show. Once more I took the Boy out of its frame and presented myself at the B.M. The curator was a ravishing blond woman in her late thirties, surrounded by a retinue of disciples. Our meeting took place in a library under a small rotunda. The Boy was placed on a table. All trooped around it, while I stood some distance away, listening to murmurs of astonishment, of admiration, of questioning. The curator turned to a young man at her side and addressed him in a low voice. He left the library and returned a few minutes later bearing a large leather-bound book. The Boy was pushed to one side of the table to make room for the folio. The curator opened it and turned the pages until she came to what she was looking for. All heads crowded around the open page. I heard urgent whisperings and the curator turned to me: "Can you take bad news?" she asked.

I approached the table. The disciples made way for me to look at the open page where I saw a black-and-white photograph of my Boy, but in true, unmistakable, classical, orthodox Fayum style. Forcefully delineated, without hint of mist or cloudy quality or graphic smudginess.

"This is the original," explained the curator. "The artist who painted yours clearly used this portrait as his guide. The original was given to the Metropolitan Museum of New York in 1914. Yours, you understand, is not a copy, was never meant to be one. It was inspired by the original, and it's remarkable. It's beautiful. We must forgive the artist for using wooden slats as if . . . but let me show you the proof that it's not a Fayum portrait." The curator gently spread out the slats of my plaque and pointed to traces of paint smudged on the thickness of the wood, paint that had clearly seeped between the slats. "The portraits are often painted on a rounded base. The Bedouins, when they find them, flatten them out, easier to transport that way, and the wood breaks into slats. At the time they're painted, of course, there are no slats, the wooden ground is solid, no paint can seep through . . ."

I trust the expression on my face showed nothing more than a scientific interest and concern for the truth. I thanked the curator, who handed me back the Boy. "Return him to his frame. Put him back where he belongs, and appreciate him as ever. Just cancel the insurance."

30

Remember to Remember

That fatidic moment I mentioned in the preface came about in a POW camp in Burma after I had translated the request of my superior officer, Lieutenant Colonel Hutchinson, to the Japanese camp commandant, an officer cadet. Overnight more men had died of beriberi, a deficiency caused by the lack of vitamin B1. Our basic nourishment was rice, of low quality and in drastically insufficient quantity. Moreover it was polished rice, that is, husked, whereas all the Vitamin B1 is found in the husks, known as "rice polishings."

Hutch, as we called him, remarked in an indignant tone that the horses of the Imperial Japanese Army were given rice polishings. Why were they denied to us? The cadet instantly fell into a dangerous and uncontrollable rage, a specifically Japanese state called *mu sekinin*, or loss of responsibility. He shouted at one of his men to fetch his sword, pulled it out of its scabbard, and screamed at us, his eyes mere slits, his mouth foaming. We were undisciplined. As prisoners we'd lost all honor, we had no right to claim anything, an example must be made, we had to die. He ordered us to kneel and bend our heads and so free our necks. "The enemies I've killed with this sword! Two more!" He took that first swipe over my head.

I had, as I said, but a few seconds to live, yet I was seized by an overbearing desire. As my head separated from my body, I wanted it to carry a noble idea—one in keeping with the event, an ultimate trace of my presence in this life. Might it be my last image of this world? With head lowered to bare the neck, eyes on the ground, all that was visible beyond Japanese boots was a strip of dark green forest. For a noble thought, I tried God. It was meaningless. In turn, like instant flashes of lightning illuminating nothing, images and ideas raced through my mind. I dismissed them all. The search stopped, and I found myself in a great void, conscious of being nothing but a receptacle for ready-made beliefs, mouthing words of no significance. I'd been granted two decades of life, a life of mimicry, and I was about to disappear. Despair, incommensurable despair, was all I felt.

•

I never alluded to that strange experience, nor did anyone ever ask me to describe what I'd felt during these moments. In prison camps, there was a sense of shame that prevented us from freely revealing our private thoughts to others—irrational thoughts that veered from hope to despair. Yet I couldn't forego or forget that moment of lucidity. I spoke to men who'd been close to death. But it was always a near death induced by disease, overwork, and starvation. No one I met had faced the imminence of a beheading and survived.

In the River Kwai work camps, we had very few books; they had been discarded on the march or used up for cigarette paper. But when, along with the survivors of the "Death Railway," I was shipped back to Singapore, I came across a copy of Ouspensky's *Tertium Organum*. I realized then I was not alone and sensed, in a vague, inchoate, and subterranean way, the value of what I'd experienced.

Shortly after my repatriation to Britain, I went to America, and on the ski slopes of New Hampshire I met a young divorced woman who had read Ouspensky. She was beautiful and eager to further my education in more ways than one. The providence that had allowed me to survive the war was apparently still in attendance. My new friend also frequented the Ramakrishna-Vivekananda Center in New York. (When I questioned her about her divorce, she told me that in bed, while she read the *Bhagavad Ghita,* her husband read *Victory Through Air Power.*) Back in New York, M. and I made love, drank a lot of bourbon, and talked about esoteric matters. Rather than the intricacies of Indian worship with its infinity of deities, I favored Ouspensky's speculations, and attended readings from his books.

Ouspensky had been a pupil of Gurdjieff, a celebrated and mysterious figure, a teacher who attracted both American and European writers, artists, and thinkers. Ouspensky was Gurdjieff's Saint Paul. His *Tertium Organum* (after Aristotle's *Organon* and Bacon's *Novum Organum*) was principally an interpretation of Gurdjieff's method and ideas which, when expounded by the master, were obscure, often deliberately so. The news was then heard that George Ivanovitch Gurdjieff himself would be coming to New York. It was to be his ultimate teaching. M. and I rushed to enroll. We didn't suspect to what extent our lives would be engulfed, colored, and influenced by this step. For ten months we attended the sessions almost every evening. Even though biographies and memoirs, along with Gurdjieff's own books, are easy to find, it's worth recalling these long soirées that started around 7:00 P.M. and ended up close to midnight.

We met at the Carnegie Dance Studios on 57th Street, next to Carnegie Hall, about fifty of us, men and women, to engage in a special form of dancing—an important part of the curriculum designed to achieve control over the body. (We all know the problem of tracing in the air a square with the right hand and simultaneously a circle with the left.) The dancing was mostly to the music of the Sufis, said to be a major influence on Gurdjieff, and to one of his closest followers, Madame de Hartmann. Gurdjieff was in no way a "mystic" as it was vulgarly said, although he probably had unusual psychological powers. He regarded science as "the entry point nowadays to the knowledge of the Universe," but the body was the laboratory, and it was up to each one of us to understand how the different functions, the centers, worked, and so conduct the proper experiments. The aim was to achieve a greater awareness, in Gurdjieff's terms, a super-consciousness—the highest, almost unreachable of three states: the first being the sleep state, and the second wakefulness. Yet, beyond super-consciousness, came the Enlightened Beings, but at any given time, the latter are extremely few, and often there are none at all.

Man is a machine and has no will: such was the crux of Gurdjieff's teaching, a notion we were enjoined always to keep in mind. Man is asleep, but he is ignorant of that fact. If you want to wake up, you first have to realize that you are asleep. Similarly, if you want to escape from prison, you need to know first that you are in prison. Moreover, you can't escape on your own; you need someone on the outside to send you a tiny saw concealed in an orange. You need a Master.

We are asleep, but we imagine we are awake. It requires a shock to break the trance. I was awake when the sword whistled over my head.

After the dances, we trooped to the Wellington Hotel, ten minutes' walk away, where Gurdjieff lived and where a number of volunteers had prepared a copious meal, mostly of Armenian, Turkish, and Central Asian food—the countries of Gurdjieff's birth and travels. We sat in the large living room

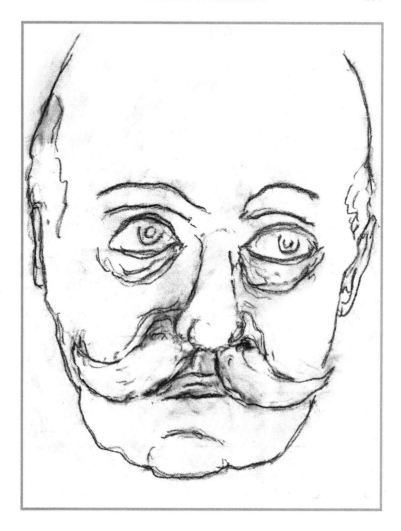

and listened to someone read from the Master's books. *Meetings with Remarkable Men* was the most understandable, although long-winded and its meaning not always clear; others such as *Beelzebub's Tales to his Grandson* were incomprehensible. As with Joyce's works, a key would have been helpful.

Readings were occasionally interrupted by Gurdjieff, a large, dark, imposing, and mysterious figure (he was then seventy-four years old), who would call for a drink to "an idiot"—idiots being different stages of mankind in its ascent toward levels of consciousness. Only Calvados was served, and you had to sink your drink in one gulp. In the course of an evening you might well go through six small tumblers of the stuff, yet I never saw anyone show signs of inebriety or sleepiness, nor did I experience the slightest effect. How was it possible, or was the Calvados watered?

Gurdjieff often interrupted the reader to expound on the subject at hand. He might be difficult to understand, or else difficult to believe. There were Laws and Rules—the Law of Seven, the Rule of Three, and above all the Fourth Way: the first being the way of the fakir, a way that requires a willpower beyond understanding (such as letting nails grow through the palm of the hand, or standing for years on one leg) but leads nowhere; the second is the way of the monk, requiring faith over knowledge, and faith can easily be misguided (concerning ritual, he compared it to people boarding a ship to reach a certain destination, and enjoying the trip so much that they forget why they got on the ship in the first place); the third way is that of the yogi who cultivates knowledge of the mind. The Fourth Way was Gurdjieff's, which took from the others but contained new and important elements of its own, specifically the proof that (a) we are machines and (b) that we cannot remember. It is extremely difficult to get the mind to focus on a single action for more than three minutes (try it while brushing your teeth), and it takes but a few moments for one's memory to disperse its contents (try to remember what you thought at breakfast). In brief, we need to remember to remember. Besides, asked Gurdjieff, "Who are you? You wake up and the sun is shining, you're happy. You wake up and it's raining, you're unhappy. You have no center of gravity."

After ten months or so of devoting all my evenings to the group, I was asked to join the so-called monastery at Mendham, in New Jersey. This was a great surprise, and apart from having to think seriously of the consequences of leaving my normal and current life for a year or so, I began to have doubts. Not about Gurdjieff and his teaching, but about the way Ouspensky's grandson, part of the New York group, was being used to demonstrate man's mechanical nature. The boy was slow-witted, and I questioned anyone's right to use a human being as a guinea pig. Indeed, Gurdjieff was adept at using people's weaknesses against themselves, but he was also charitable—acquiring bad paintings, for instance, from impoverished artists in order not to humiliate them by simply giving them money. Maybe I misread what was going on with the Ouspensky boy, but it led me to intense questioning.

At dinners given by a very Catholic lady in Manhattan, I'd met a young priest, a typical *abbé de salon*, good-looking, amusing, and worldly. He was Egyptian, a convert from an ancient Jewish family settled in Alexandria for two millennia. He had spent time at the Vatican, and when I knew him he was the curate of a parish in a small New Jersey township. Why he'd been assigned to such a place I don't know, but it's unlikely that the Vatican fathers foresaw the Catholic ladies of the Upper East side sending their limousines and chauffeurs to pick him up for their dinner parties and then late in the evening drive him back to Jersey. I approached him after one of my Catholic dinners and told him about my year with Gurdjieff and my quandary about staying or leaving. "I know about him," he said. "Simply listen to your own devil."

I declined the invitation to Mendham and left the Gurdjieff group. I still try to remember.

31

HCB in the Luberon

enri Cartier-Bresson. I've already told how, thanks to him, I discovered that I had a talent for photography. And also thanks to him I discovered the Luberon, that blessed part of Provence, green Provence, the French Tuscany. HCB's house, in old days a farm, stands on the side of a hill, from which you contemplate in the distance more hills—not quite mountains—and look down on a vast *mosaique* of grass, wheat, and lavender fields, of flocks of sheep and rows of poplars to protect the fields from the mistral, the wind that (too often) comes roaring down the Rhône Valley. Far too much has been written about Provence, and I'll say no more about it. However, I owe its discovery to Henri, and for the past twenty-five years this is where I've been summering, renting houses (until I had my own) close to his, beyond the town of Apt and the village of Céreste. This suited him well because he refused to have a swimming pool, believing that the water was turned on 365 days a year, an abysmal waste. I explained that it was not so. He passed no comment and used my pool.

HCB had a tunnel view of photography: when shown pictures that were not photojournalism, he'd admit they had an affinity with the skills and techniques of photography, but no more. Of my own work I've heard him say, "You call it photography, but it doesn't mean much to me." Yet, after I'd sent him a book I had compiled on folds and draperies,* a book that had required over two years of work and travel to far places, he did write (in English), "I did not know you were a gentleman-photographer producing palpitating still-lives." In spite of that letter, he once told a Japanese friend from New York, an art dealer, that she should represent my drawings rather than my photographic work. Occasionally Henri and I went off driving, selected a landscape, and, sitting on our folding stools ten or twenty yards apart, we would draw for hours without exchanging a word.

HCB had strong views about the changes that had affected the Luberon, changes mostly due, according to him, to the presence of "foreigners" who bought old houses, châteaux, farms, barns, watermills, and even byres, and turned them into "secondary homes" as the French call them. For HCB there were two kinds of foreigners, those born outside France and those born outside Provence—like himself who claimed Norman origins. "We have no business being here, neither you nor I," he once said, eyeing me at lunch. The mayor of Montjustin, a tiny village close to Henri's house, was present at that lunch and went pale. He was most likely projecting the abysmal financial collapse if foreigners of all breeds were to be exiled from the Luberon.

Henri often lost his temper when the conversation didn't go his way. During one of these outbursts he shouted, "Anyway there's only one person at this table who understands what I'm saying. It's John, who like me is a Buddhist and an anarchist!" Martine Franck, his wonderful wife and also a great photographer, called him "*un Bouddhiste agité*," a busybody Buddhist.

---

* *Gravitas*, Azimuth Editions, London, 1988.

Despite all his quirks and sometimes his aggressiveness, HCB was a profoundly kind man. He was also childlike, and that characteristic was both the clue to his seemingly irrational behavior and the reason he was so lovable. When alone with him, you knew that he had a special hold of the present, a grasp, a focus, so that nothing in the world mattered but that moment between you and him. It was, I thought, as astonishing as the way an infant grasps your finger, with such strength and determination.

This immediacy of feeling was replicated in his immediacy of vision. There was no way it could be taught. A woman related to me that once she was in a car with Henri at the wheel. (He was a bad and fearsome driver.) They were following a country road when HCB saw a landscape that he thought worth recording. He didn't have his camera, or else it was out of reach, so he took both hands off the wheel, brought them up to his eye as if holding his camera, turned sideways toward the landscape and mimicked with his right thumb and index the clicking of the shutter, without of course bothering to slow down. That story reminded me of the old and famous Japanese master of archery who never missed hitting the bull's eye on the target. He was asked how he did it. "I imagine the target and then I shoot," said the master. Henri—who when asked by people the way to improve their photography always advised them to read Eugen Herrigel's *Zen in the Art of Archery*—would have loved that story. Alas, I heard it told long after he had left us for the minute cemetery of Montjustin where his remains lie under a simple stone, a small cypress at its head, and two olive trees: one planted there by the members of Magnum, the photo agency Henri started with Robert Capa; the other by the inhabitants of Montjustin.

32

Coda

Finally, this is the kind of courage that is demanded
—to have courage for the strongest, the most singular
and the most inexplicable that we might ever encounter.

Rainer Maria Rilke

His life was unraveling. Alex, my younger son, had been fighting leukemia for two years. After two chemotherapies in Paris, his doctors had recommended that he go back to New York, where the hospital protocols would permit experimental treatments. Nothing worked.

Those were bad times, once relieved by the publication of his first novel* when his nurses at Sloan-Kettering Hospital posted the press reviews on their bulletin-boards: a writer was in their midst, a teller of tales. They bought his book and asked him to inscribe it for them.

I learned from his friends that he was worried about what would happen to me after his death. How would I pick up the threads? I'd sat at his side ever since the terrible disease had

---

*Alex Ullmann, *Afghanistan*, Ticknor & Fields, New York, 1992. Awarded the prize for the Best First Novel of 1992 by the American Academy of Arts and Letters.

appeared, as close to a son as a father can be. Alex invariably showed concern for his friends, never mentioning his own ordeal. They were all in dumb admiration, ashamed to have mentioned before him their mean troubles, their pusillanimous problems.

I came to the hospital one morning, as I did every day around 10 A.M. Alex was lying on his back, his glasses on his nose, staring at the ceiling. He turned his head as I entered the room, smiled, and asked how I'd slept. Not well, I told him.

"Not surprising," he said.

"Alex, I'll reveal something to you, something I've never told anyone. Absolutely no one. Ever since I was a boy, at those times when I have trouble falling asleep—and you know I've been blessed with a wonderful ability for sleep—I imagine that I'm on my sailboat, lying in my bunk. I listen to the sound of waves lapping against the hull, and their rhythm lulls me to sleep."

"Your bunk, is it port or starboard?" asked Alex.

"Why do you ask? Starboard."

"Because I do the same, exactly the same. On starboard as well."

Now I have nothing more to tell you.

LIST OF ILLUSTRATIONS